THE TRAGEDY OF IGNORING THE CREATOR

The

TRAGEDY *of*

IGNORING

the

CREATOR

And Other Essays on
Christian Life and Ministry

MAURICE R. IRVIN

CHRISTIAN PUBLICATIONS

CAMP HILL, PENNSYLVANIA

Christian Publications
3825 Hartzdale Drive, Camp Hill, PA 17011

Faithful, biblical publishing since 1883

ISBN: 0-87509-575-5
© 1995 by Christian Publications
All rights reserved
Printed in the United States of America

95 96 97 98 99   5 4 3 2 1

CONTENTS

Foreword

There are crimes of passion and crimes of logic. The entailments are disastrous if at any time in history the two combine and enter the mindset of any culture. Few can escape the consequences when subjected to that fatal mix. With burgeoning populations in our cities and increasing pluralization, crimes of passion seem inescapable. Society, at least at face value, makes an attempt to etch laws into its social conscience and to erect structures to police such laws that we might render judgments upon those whose criminality is established. As innocuous as such meager solutions seem to be in dealing with untamed passions, the cities of men offer no better answers in search of the best of all possible worlds.

Of far greater consequence, however, are crimes of logic; for in the violation of reason, the very facility by which we judge truth, beauty and goodness is impoverished.

Few social critics of our time will deny the cultural chaos that has overtaken most modern societies, particularly in the West. While words such as "ethics" or "values" proliferate our innumerable talk shows, the words of the Apostle Paul come to mind as most suitably describing the abundance of talk and the paucity of meaning. He spoke of a people who were forever learning but never able to come to a knowledge of the truth. The constant debate on values comes from quarters where cultural elites are more prone to debunk the notion of absolutes either in their works, which masquerade under the vacuous category of the arts, or by espoused lifestyles that mock the idea of anything sacred.

This schizophrenia, or talk of values bereft of any moral point of reference, was poignantly captured by Os Guinness in his book *The American Hour*, in which he states that "Just say no" has become America's most urgent slogan at the very moment when "Why not?" has become America's most publicly unanswerable question. And so it is that when we open our newspapers each day we read page after page of passion run amok in the lives of so many. As discouraging as the stories of victim after victim may be, the greater disappointment is found on the editorial pages where no relief is offered in analyses and solutions that defy even common sense.

In the midst of such drastic foundational shifts, as so-called experts interpret the times, the Christian often finds himself or herself quite bewildered, swinging between the Scylla of defeatism and the Charybdis of hyper-activism. Our reactions swerve from apathy (a form of paralysis) to untempered rage (a vision without wisdom). Neither of these extremes will do, for the one abdicates responsibility, awaiting the trumpet sound, while the other resorts to methods that malign the very message which supposedly motivated the response.

It may be of little comfort to all of us standing upon such cultural quicksand to be reminded of Malcolm Muggeridge's words offered to every generation. "All new news," said he, "is old news happening to new people." But it is worth remembering that our modern crisis is not without precedent. From the days of the demise of Greek civilization and of the tarnishing of Roman glory or, for that matter, the tragic spiritual collapse of Israel, human passion propelled by unreason has taken its toll. Today in those cultures even the stones speak of structures and laws that brought down the cities of men. We would do well to read again how Augustine wept bitterly as he heard the news of Rome's collapse, and then penned his masterpiece *The City of God.* Our Lord Himself wept over Jerusalem, for He saw more clearly than anyone else the utter tragedy when a people squandered the things that belonged unto their peace.

But in all that such spiritually dark times portend, the Word of God has always called the people of God to a different focus than the God-denying minds that seem ever gullible to swallow another quick-fix potion. Their solutions repeatedly seem to point to some new idea, to some newly elected official or to some new program to usher in the utopia. In no uncertain terms God always appeals first to His people to search their own hearts and set their own houses in order. It is those who are called by

His name whom He beckons to humble themselves. It is in the house of the Lord that Josiah's officials found the book of the law that had been buried under the dust and rubble of temple politics.

It is to this recovery and this focus that Maurice Irvin brings his pen, blending the legitimacy of passion and the power of sound reasoning. His genius in Scriptural exposition, a God-given gift, brings a cogent analysis of the issues that confront us. His breadth of study and depth of insight lead us back to the only timeless truth, the sacred Scriptures, without which even the best of passion and the soundest of reasoning become all sail and no anchor. As he wrestles with contemporary issues, be they in the public arena or in ecclesiastical debate, we are constantly reminded that there is not merely a right or a left perspective ideologically but an up and a down perspective theologically.

I cannot resist but add one more distinctive that his writings bring. The demand of an editorial is not merely one of content or intent, it is also one of conciseness. Maurice Irvin reveals extraordinary strength in meeting this challenge, for here one meets enormous truths presented in succinct beauty—an enviable gift.

I commend these writings not just for the information they contain, but for the inspiration they evoke. The imperative will soon become clear that spiritual force is different from any other force, but it has its own way of conquering. There is clearly a call to the Church to let this mind be in us which was also in Christ—to be in the world, but not of it; to be reflective of His glory and confident of His triumph, as human utopias crumble. Ideas have consequences, and the ideas presented here can engender zeal and knowledge of the right kind to rescue us from spurious alternatives.

Dr. Ravi Zacharias
January 1995

Preface

The essays in this volume originally appeared as editorials in *Alliance Life* magazine between 1989 and 1994. They are intended to be thought-provoking discussions of topics related to Christian life and ministry. This is a companion volume to a similar collection published in 1989 under the title *Consider This: Thoughts for the Serious Christian.*

On several occasions I have been asked where I get ideas for editorials. (I produce about 20 such essays a year in addition to other writing assignments.)

Some editorials present insights that I gained or convictions I developed during the 31 years I spent in pastoral ministries. It would have been hard for me not to have learned some valuable truths during all of those multiplied hours I spent in prayerful study between 1952 and 1983.

A lot of the opinions I put into editorials come from my observations of current conditions, especially the current religious scene. While I am now primarily an editor and spend a lot of my time sitting behind a desk, I travel a great deal. Last year I spoke nearly 100 times in churches, conferences and schools. I visited more than 15 states and provinces in the United States and Canada and seven foreign countries. A person cannot be exposed to so many different situations without feeling compelled to comment on some of the things he sees.

Also, I read a lot. I consume books while traveling and sometimes read at home. What other people say in print stimulates my thinking and teaches me things I try to pass on through my writings to others.

I also like to think that some of the things I write have come directly from the Lord. On occasion, as I have sat down to write, words have seemed almost to flow through me onto the paper. I hope that at least some of the ideas set forth in the essays contained in this book can be recognized as more than simply human opinions.

Quite a few of the essays in this book concern the contemporary church. I make no apology for this. The church remains the primary organism through which God carries on His work in the world. Every Christian should be concerned that the church be pure and strong, and every believer should be committed to its ministry.

These essays can be read devotionally, perhaps one a day in connection with Bible reading and prayer. They can be used as discussion starters in small group meetings or for Sunday school class sessions. I hope they will provoke fellow Christians to think carefully about the issues that I have raised.

I wish to express my appreciation to members of the *Alliance Life* editorial staff, particularly to Mike Saunier, Doug Wicks and Dena Eastman. They freely have expressed their opinions to me concerning things that I have written, and they have helped to edit my work. Also, they each had a major role in the production of this book.

I also thank Dr. Ravi Zacharias for contributing a thoughtful foreword to this volume.

Maurice R. Irvin
January 1995

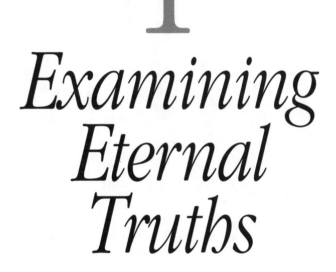

1
Examining Eternal Truths

The Tragedy of Ignoring the Creator

I like to watch nature programs on television: *National Geographic* specials, "Wild America," "The Wild World of Animals" and the like. Such programs explore the amazing diversity that exists in plant life across the globe. There are, I have been told, 350,000 different kinds of plants and 250,000 varieties of flowers.

These nature programs often reveal the remarkable diversity of living things that exists in the earth's oceans, from microscopic plankton to massive whales. They profile some of the more than one million species of animals and birds that fill the earth's forests, plains and mountains. I am fascinated by the incredible ways in which these creatures have adapted to their environment. I am astounded by some of their unusual behaviors.

All these things testify to the glory of their Creator. Creation is an enormous mirror that reflects the wisdom, power and ingenuity of the God who made all things. Over and over as I watch these programs, I am impressed by how clearly they declare God's glory. Passages of Scripture come to my mind, like Psalm 104:24, "How many are your works, O LORD! / In wisdom you made them all; / the earth is full of your creatures."

Yet not one of the programs ever gives God any credit for what He has created; none ever acknowledges God's hand in His universe.

Romans 1:20 says, "For since the creation of the world God's invisible qualities—his eternal power and divine nature—have been clearly seen, being understood from what has been made." But the next verse in Romans says, concerning people on this earth, "For although they knew God, they neither glorified him as God nor gave thanks to him, but their thinking became futile and their foolish hearts were darkened."

This is exactly true of the natural scientists and the script writers who are behind the nature programs on television. When attempting to account for the dazzling beauty, the phenomenal diversity, the amazing behaviors they find in creation, they say, "Evolution has produced this" or "Nature has caused this." Never even once has anyone on any program I have watched ever said, "God made this, and He deserves honor for His glorious wisdom and power."

It is a pity that men are so determined to avoid God that they refuse to see the Creator in His creation. How pleased Satan must be to see the Lord ignored right in the midst of the bounty and beauty He has supplied. How sad that children and youth who see such programs are so consistently fed distorted information concerning the origins of things. How it must grieve God when He has so clearly stamped His signature upon the canvas of creation that foolish men will not honor Him for what He has made.

Sir Francis Bacon said, "While the mind of man looketh upon second causes scattered, it may sometimes rest in them and go no further, but, when it beholdeth the chain of them confederate and linked together, it must needs fly to Providence and Deity" (*Essay on Atheism*). Sir Isaac Newton, probably the smartest man who ever lived (apart from Jesus), unhesitatingly attributed all the processes and laws in nature to a divine Creator. John Stuart Mill wrote, "The adaptations in nature afford a large balance of probability in favor of causation by intelligence" (*Three Essays on Theism*).

But in our so-called enlightened age people are so blind to the obvious that they cannot see God in His creation.

Long ago a very wise man said, "Where there is no vision, the people perish" (Proverbs 29:18, KJV). Russia is busy trying to put some vision of God back into its nation to stem the social and political disintegration taking place there. North Americans are busy removing any consciousness of God from national life, and this will lead (indeed, it already has led) to tragic consequences for society.

Someone Is in Control

The main highway leading into downtown Pittsburgh, Pennsylvania, from the south comes down Greentree Hill. In the past some trucks on that steep grade have lost their brakes, gone out of control and crashed. One truck, several years ago, roared down that hill, went through a tunnel, crossed a bridge, entered a congested downtown street and finally smashed into the side of one of the city's leading department stores.

Sometimes it seems as if human history has become a runaway truck plunging down a steep grade. In recent years momentous changes have taken place across our globe. Thousands of refugees surged across the border from East Germany into the West, and the Berlin Wall was torn down. The dictator of Romania was executed, and the Soviet Union collapsed. And all these things happened with incredible speed. Not long ago a Greek lawyer whom I met in an airport in Guatemala said, "Things are changing too fast, much too fast. Human affairs are out of control."

Revelation 5 sets before us another perspective on the culmination of human history. That chapter takes us into the throne room of heaven. There we see God, the Father, seated upon His throne of glory. He holds in His hand a scroll, and as we watch a Lamb steps forth to take the scroll from the Father and begins to unroll it.

The scroll represents God's blueprint for the consummation of human history. William Barclay has written:

> There is no doubt that the book [scroll] is the book of divine decrees; it is the book of the destinies of the world; it contains the record of that which is to happen in the last times; it is, if we like to put it so, the book of history written in advance.

The opening of that scroll signifies control over what is to transpire in the last days upon the earth. And the Lamb who

17

takes the scroll to unroll it is Jesus Christ. So Revelation 5 affirms to us that Jesus Christ will take charge of human affairs. If history indeed has become like a runaway truck plunging down a steep grade, Revelation 5 assures us that Christ will move into the cab, take over the wheel, apply the brakes and direct that truck to the destination that God has purposed for it.

Christ is set forth in Revelation 5 as having seven eyes and seven horns. Seven in the Bible stands for completion or perfection. Eyes symbolize wisdom. So the Christ who takes control of the consummation of human history has perfect wisdom, complete understanding. The world through the centuries has been torn apart by conflicting ideologies. It has suffered tragically from the effects of human follies. Thank God final destinies and ultimate decisions will be determined by One who has right answers and perfect solutions.

The seven horns represent perfect and complete power. And thank God the One who has all power will control the end of the age. This earth staggers under the weight of monumental problems: crime, pollution, starvation, racial hatreds, regional conflicts, wars, violence, corruption, ignorance, injustice. Only One possessing all power can finally resolve all these issues.

And the One who is set forth in Revelation 5 as the Lord of future history is a lamb. Verse 9 says, "You were slain, / and with your blood you purchased men for God."

This is the posture Christ assumed during His life on earth. He said, "The Son of Man did not come to be served, but to serve, and to give his life as a ransom for many" (Matthew 20:28). He pours Himself out even now as "he always lives to intercede for [us]" (Hebrews 7:25). He will still be the Lamb, pouring out His life to redeem, restore, deliver and heal those who will come to God by Him.

We often stress that the end times will usher in judgments, but the character of His ultimate government of human affairs is conditioned by His desire to redeem.

The upheavals taking place across the globe may fill us with apprehension. But Revelation 5 assures us that Jesus Christ reigns over the consummation of the ages, and that is better news than anything we will ever read in our newspapers.

A New World Order

A few years ago politicians were hailing the emergence of "a new world order." At the time it seemed an appropriate term to describe the global scene. Germany was reunited. Oppressive Communist regimes were overthrown in Eastern Europe. The cold war seemed ended.

Then the old world order reappeared. Civil war broke out in several African countries. Russia began using force against breakaway republics. Repression, conflict, destruction and death are again the order of the day.

Sadly, we are faced with the fact that man does not have the capacity to establish peace and justice throughout the earth. "The war to end all wars," "a world safe for democracy," "the Great Society," "the Age of Aquarius," "a new world order"—all have become empty expressions of unfulfilled aspirations.

The problem is the essential depravity of human nature. Enough of the naive optimism of the early 1900s lingers to cause people to resent talk about evil within human beings. We still want to harbor romantic notions about people being essentially good.

But the records of human conduct all too clearly confirm the teaching of theologians who say all men by nature are inclined to evil. (John R. W. Stott in *Basic Christianity* speaks of "a deep-seated, inward corruption" and of a "moral disease" within.) Ultimately, violence on our streets, widespread drug abuse, corruption in business and government, war and all the rest that is wrong around us stem from the selfishness, greed, pride, dishonesty and lust ingrained in human nature.

A genuinely new world order, then, will come about only when people are changed within, when their basic human dispositions are transformed.

When Christ went to the cross, He took the power of human sin into Himself. And He broke that power; He rose from the grave triumphant over sin. And He lives now to impart the power of His risen life into those who repent of their sinfulness and trust in Him as Savior. He gives to people who receive Him as Savior the ability to live good lives, to treat others properly and to honor God as we ought. A genuinely new world order can come about only through people made new creatures in Christ Jesus.

Obviously, however, what I have stated above is an overly simplistic solution to the world's ills. Even those who receive Christ as Savior do not always thereafter do only good. We can fail to allow the power of Christ to operate as fully within us as we should and therefore still, to a degree, be a part of the problem. Moreover, a great many people in our world refuse to allow Christ to become their Savior and thus are not changed by His power.

Christians emphasize, therefore, not only the truth that Christ can come by His Spirit to the human heart to change people from the inside out. We also joyously proclaim that He is going to return, visibly and personally, to this earth again.

When Jesus Christ was crucified, He confronted all the power of all the evil in the world. Hell's forces were set against Him. The greatest political power in the world of that day tried to keep Him in the grave. And He conquered it all in His Resurrection. Thus He remains today as a living Lord with supreme power over all His foes.

The Scriptures clearly teach that He will come again to earth to perfect the salvation of those who have trusted in Him. As well He will cast down those who set themselves against God's holy purposes for this earth. He forcefully will put an end to crime and cruelty, conflict and confusion. He will cause all wars to cease and will banish all corruption.

Then, finally, when the victory of Christ's Resurrection is fully implemented in all those who remain on the earth and over all nations and institutions, we will indeed see a new world order.

Troubling Uncertainties about Salvation

I once heard a Christian testify, "From the day I trusted in Christ as my Savior until now"—and this was for him a period of many years—"I have never had one moment of uncertainty about my salvation."

When I heard that, I found myself envying that man. I have had moments of uncertainty. I still have them.

My insignificance troubles me. We live in a universe of mind-boggling vastness. Our earth in this universe is like one tiny grain of sand on a huge beach. And I am less than a microscopic speck on that minuscule particle. How can a God who has this enormous universe spread out before Him possibly care about something so utterly inconsequential as me?

My unworthiness causes me to doubt. God is absolutely holy, indescribably radiant, full of ineffable glory. People like Isaiah who saw glimpses of God's splendor were stricken with an overwhelming sense of their sinfulness. I wonder how God can possibly even look at someone so entirely imperfect and impotent as me. These and other mysteries attack my sense of assurance.

I have no way of knowing how many other Christians may have doubts as I do. We do not generally talk about our uncertainties. But I suspect I am not alone in possessing at times less than an untroubled heart.

This problem of uncertainty about our salvation is compounded for some of us by erroneous notions about the meaning of faith. Many think faith is believing hard that something is so. If I am sick I must believe very hard that I am well. And that is said (by some people) to be exercising faith.

Such a concept ruins a doubter. That idea of faith produces this kind of thinking: Salvation depends upon faith (Ephesians 2:8; Romans 1:17). Faith is believing hard that something is so. At times I cannot make myself believe I am saved. Therefore, I must not really be a Christian.

Thank God faith is not believing hard that something is so. Faith is utter reliance upon God. Therefore my salvation does not depend upon my ability to believe it is true but upon God's ability to ransom me from my sin and reconcile me to Himself. When I throw myself upon God's mercy and trust in what Christ has done for me, I am saved whether I am certain about it or not, whether or not I *feel* saved.

Thank God my doubts about my worthiness do not destroy my relationship with Him. "If our heart condemn us, God is greater than our heart" (1 John 3:20, KJV). Our salvation does not depend upon our being able to understand it. Our eternal redemption depends upon God's infinite grace.

I am very aware that the Spirit bears witness with our spirits that we are the children of God. I have had such a witness within my soul. Happy indeed is the person to whom that witness is constant.

But for me—and, I think, for others—that witness sometimes fades. Clouds obscure that sweet sunshine to the soul. Perhaps we sometimes let the world's voices drown out the voice of the Spirit.

We do not have to be sure every moment that we are saved in order to be saved. Our deliverance from condemnation and possession of eternal life depends upon the great God who promises to save us if we trust Him.

These comments will mean nothing to those people who walk in untroubled, unbroken assurance. I write this because I believe some Christians feel condemned by their uncertainties.

In my confusion, I simply throw myself all the more completely upon the Lord. And I urge any of my fellow doubters to do so, too.

With or without assurance, whether we can understand or not, we must cling to Christ, stand on God's mercy and keep persevering.

The Resurrection's
Greatest Reward

Reflecting on the Christian's unique privilege of personal fellowship with Jesus Christ, John Newton wrote:

His Name yields the richest perfume,
And sweeter than music His voice;
His presence disperses my gloom,
And makes all within me rejoice.

Because Christ rose from the dead, such sweet, soul-enriching fellowship is available to every child of God.

Jesus is alive. As a living being He thinks and feels and speaks and moves. Thus we can talk to Him, commune as person to person and hear Him speak.

And because He is the altogether lovely One, full of grace and truth, the fairest of ten thousand, we can find in Him life's greatest satisfaction and purest joy. We can behold no greater beauty, look upon no more dazzling light, enjoy no more enriching presence, bow before no greater majesty.

Yet few Christians enter into the intimate fellowship and rich experiences of personal communion with Christ that are possible for them. Most of us spend about as much time each day in the presence of Jesus as we spend with our country's president or prime minister. Jesus is about as real to us as some fictional character in a novel we have read, and we know Him about like we know one of the persons who reports the evening news.

In part, present-day preaching and teaching is responsible for leading us away from personal fellowship with Christ. Much of it encourages us to seek His blessings instead of desiring Him. We are told that God means for us to be wealthy and well. Indeed, prosperity and wholeness are signs of God's favor. So we are to claim greater material possessions and pursue increased levels of personal comfort.

As a result we sing a revised version of Dr. A. B. Simpson's hymn: "Once it was the Lord; now it is the blessing." Instead of seeking to be seated in the heavenlies, we want to sit in a Cadillac. Paul's great prayer "That I may know Him" has become "That I may be happy." And consumed with the benefits of salvation, we miss the Savior.

As well we fail to enter into the experience of intimate communion with our Lord because of the contemporary emphasis on activity. A. W. Tozer once wrote, "It takes time to know God." Henri Nouwen has said, "It is impossible to be spiritual without solitude." Yet the average Christian is almost never still. When we come home we immediately turn on the TV. Every 15 minutes the phone rings. Work days are crowded with responsibility. Every member of the household has three dozen things to do. Weekends are filled to capacity. Vacations are a whirl of activities.

Church activities demand much of our free time. We have lessons to prepare, committee meetings to attend and salads to make for the church supper. We must take the kids to their meetings and go to our group's get-together.

And Christ? Yes, we trust Him and love Him, but we cannot quite fit Him into our schedule. He is like that book we got for Christmas that we somehow cannot find time to read. So our risen, living Lord remains outside the inner circle of our deepest desires and greatest concerns.

Bernard of Clairvaux wrote:

Jesus, highest heaven's completeness,
  Name of music to the ear,
To the lips surpassing sweetness,
  Wine the fainting heart to cheer.

Eating Thee, the soul may hunger,
  Drinking, still athirst may be;
But for earthly food no longer,
  Nor for any stream but Thee.

How tragically distant is this description from most of present-day Christian experience. But because that is the case, we are robbing ourselves of one of the greatest rewards of His Resurrection—a living, personal fellowship with Him.

Are We Ready for Heaven?

Some time ago, a Gallup poll reported that 78 percent of Americans believe in heaven and that there is a good chance they will go there when they die. I am not surprised by those numbers; North Americans tend to hold romantic notions about their eternal destiny.

However, when I observe the attitudes and actions of the average American, I have to conclude that he will be utterly unprepared for what he finds there should he make it to the celestial city. In fact, I wonder if the average Christian who confidently sings, "When the roll is called up yonder, I'll be there," realizes what he will encounter "up yonder."

Admittedly, we are not told much about the exact nature of the realms above. Yet one thing is certain: individuals will have a face-to-face, personal and enduring encounter there with Almighty God. The creatures in heaven whom we see in Revelation 4 are in the presence of a radiant Being seated on a rainbow-encircled throne. The multitudes and angels in chapter 7 stand around God's throne. In every scene of heaven unfolded in Revelation, the beings are before God and respond to Him.

This is the exalted, eternal God, whose glory caused Moses' face to shine with a glow that hurt the eyes of others. This is the august Majesty before whose vision Isaiah cried, "Woe to me! I am ruined" (6:5). This is the Sovereign whose glory drove the priests from the Old Testament temple (2 Chronicles 5:14) and whose splendor overwhelmed Ezekiel (3:23).

Throughout the Book of Revelation we see the inhabitants of heaven falling down before the Lord and casting down their crowns before Him (4:6–11; 7:9–12; 19:1–8). The beings there are filled with wonder and awe and reverence. Moreover, they find all their delight and satisfaction in the Lord. Their attention is focused entirely upon Him. They sing of almost nothing else (5:9–14; 11:15–18; 15:3–4).

25

I have heard people speculate that we are told relatively little about the exact nature of heaven because the human mind cannot comprehend its glories. However, it may be that the writers of Scripture felt that all other information about heaven is irrelevant. To them it was enough to know that God Himself is there. Frederick Faber wrote of God's majesty:

Splendours upon splendours beaming
Change and intertwine;
Glories over glories streaming
All translucent shine.

Perhaps John the Revelator told us little else about what he saw when he looked into heaven because God's great radiance utterly overshadowed all else.

But is this the kind of heaven the average person anticipates and is prepared for? On every hand we see irreverence. People are careless about God's Name and His Day and His Word. Even Christians approach worship with an appalling casualness and a shocking familiarity.

And few here on earth find God to be their supreme source of joy and satisfaction. I am reminded again of what Faber wrote:

Only to sit and think of God,
Oh what a joy it is!
To think the thought, to breathe the Name
Earth has no higher bliss!

That is miles above the average Christian's appreciation of the Lord. The Barna Research Group reports that only 34 percent of the people in America who consider themselves to be Christians worship God regularly in church at least once a week.

We sing, "When all my labors and trials are o'er / And I am safe on that beautiful shore, / Just to be near the dear Lord I adore / Will through the ages be glory for me." But unless our attitudes toward the Lord and our appreciation of Him change greatly, heaven may be more of a shock than a glory. Clearly, heaven is a place of humble reverence and a place where people are totally absorbed with the Lord. We hardly are ready to spend eternity there until those attitudes are a part of our lives.

Is the Stage Set
for the Antichrist?

During a recent newscast, an authority on Eastern European affairs made a comment that caused red flags to pop up in my mind. He said that all of Eastern Europe is particularly susceptible at the moment to the emergence of some strong, charismatic leader. The collapse of ideologies, the fall of former rulers and the current political confusion invite a powerful leader to step into the present leadership vacuum.

One also could assert that all of Europe is crying for strong leadership. The European Economic Community has brought the nations of Western Europe into a political and economic unity they have not known since the days of the Roman Empire. Yet, the new alliance seems handicapped by the lack of a strong, compelling leader to carry it forward.

The Bible clearly prophesies the Antichrist's appearance at the end of the age. He apparently will rise to power in Europe. His coming, we are told, "will be in accordance with the work of Satan displayed in all kinds of counterfeit miracles, signs and wonders" (2 Thessalonians 2:9). He will gain ascendancy over every tribe, people, language and nation and will be worshiped by all the earth (Revelation 13:7–8).

However, he will be Antichrist, a substitute for the one God has appointed ruler over all things, Jesus Christ. He will set himself up in God's temple, proclaiming himself to be God (2 Thessalonians 2:4), He will make war against the saints in order to crush them (Revelation 13:7). And his aggression against the followers of the true God will help to precipitate the return of Christ to the earth to overthrow the Antichrist "with the breath of his mouth" and to destroy him "by the splendor of his coming" (2 Thessalonians 2:8).

Could the present chaos in Europe and the economic instability in the Western world have set the stage for his appearance?

In 1965 *Christianity Today* published a story written in 1900 by a Russian author named Vladimir Solovyov. In this work Solovyov portrays the rise of the Antichrist. This writer said:

> *There lived at that time a remarkable man—many called him a superman. . . . He was young, but his genius made him widely famous as a great thinker, writer and social worker by the time he was 33. . . . Soon after the publication of his book,* The Open Way to Universal Peace and Welfare, *which made its author the most popular man in the world, there was held in Berlin in the international constituent assembly of the European States Union. The delegates decided to concentrate executive power in the hands of one person, investing him with sufficient authority. The man of the future was elected, almost unanimously, lifelong president of the United States of Europe. When he appeared on the rostrum in all the brilliance of his superhuman youth and beauty and, with inspired eloquence, expounded his social program, the assembly, charmed and completely carried away in a burst of enthusiasm, decided without putting it to a vote to pay him the highest tribute by electing him Roman Emperor.*

If Solovyov's depiction is even close to being accurate, one easily could imagine this man coming to power in our day. There perhaps never has been a more propitious moment than now.

In the past some prophetic teachers have set forth dogmatic interpretations of certain biblical prophecies, including ones about the identity of the Antichrist, that have turned out to be wrong. Some teachers were sure Mussolini was this false Christ. Others were sure Hitler or one of the Popes was this one who the Bible says will appear. Some, assigning the numerical value 666 to his name, were sure Henry Kissinger was the Antichrist.

But these unwise and inaccurate assertions must not blind us to the possibility that the real Antichrist may be alive and on the earth now. And if that is the case, the end is near. No one can be sure where the present chaos will lead us, but it may be to the rapid ending of this age and the Second Advent of Christ.

An Answer
to Death

Death! It is, from an earthly perspective, so utterly and irrevocably *final.* The automobile careens out of control or the cancer sucks out the last bit of vitality or the heart feebly flutters and then stops. And life is gone.

Someone screams. Doctors work frantically. Loved ones stand by aching with a desire to reach out and grasp that life to keep it from departing. But it goes. And we can do nothing to bring it back. All the grief crowded into the following days and nights changes nothing. That life is over, finished, done, gone.

Death is so completely *destructive.* The archaeologist uncovers an ancient village. There, 3,000 or so years ago, living human beings provided for themselves food and clothing and shelter. Children played in the village streets, women met in the market and men went together into the nearby forests to hunt wild game. Now all that is left is a few broken pieces of pottery, some building stones and a half-dozen arrowheads.

We visit the ruins of an ancient palace where thousands of slaves erected a massive edifice, where some monarch lived in splendor and hoarded fabulous amounts of gold and jewels. But all the miserable lives of the slaves have ended. The proud prince has passed off the stage of history also, and only a few historians even know his name.

Some time ago I visited the Chapel of the Bones in Evora, Portugal. Years earlier, excavation at that site uncovered a mass grave where the victims of some war or plague were buried. Now the walls and pillars and ceiling of that sizable chapel are made entirely of these human skulls and bones—the remains of thousands of people who wanted to live but are entirely gone. And not one other trace of the lives of any of them remains, not even their names.

Death is such an *awesome* prospect. We strive to get a nice home. We gather around us a family. We achieve a fulfilling career or a successful business. We have a nice circle of friends. We have plans, dreams. We have so much more we want to do before we pass on.

But we are going to leave it all behind. The career will end. The family circle will be broken. We will not do all we want to do. We will die.

Death makes life seem ultimately so *futile*, so meaningless. We live hard to have and to hold, to love, to see, to know. We live to be. Death ends it all.

Our hearts cry out within each one of us, "There must be more than this!" Death cannot be the final end. If this is all there is to our existence, life is a cruel joke. If death is the ultimate victor, all our dreams, aspirations and efforts have been the delusions of fools.

Thank God there is a hereafter. This is not some fantasy created to satisfy our cravings after immortality. This is fact revealed to us by the Lord.

Its basis and proof is the Resurrection of Jesus Christ from the dead. Christian F. Gellert said it this way:

Jesus lives, and so shall I.
   Death, thy sting is gone forever.
He who deigned for me to die,
   Lives the bands of death to sever.
He shall raise me with the just:
   Jesus is my hope and trust.

Jesus lives, and death is now
   But my entrance into glory.
Courage, then my soul, for thou
   Hast a crown of life before thee;
Thou shalt find thy hopes were just.
   Jesus is the Christian's trust.

2

*Considering
Personal
Issues*

Rights or Responsibilities?

Civil rights, animal rights, gay rights, prisoners' rights, the right of a woman to choose—one cannot fail to notice the emphasis on individual rights in our society.

What one does not hear, however, is a corresponding concern about responsibility, and you cannot have one without the other.

Marriage partners insist they have the right to be happy. But they also have a responsibility to honor the commitments they made to each other. Workers have a right to fair wages and safe and comfortable working conditions. But they also have a responsibility to work hard and to produce a good product. Citizens have a right to expect government to ensure the availability of health care and other necessary social services. But they cannot escape a responsibility to pay for what they receive. Couples who engage in sex that results in a pregnancy cannot evade responsibility before God for the human being they have created.

Yet everywhere in our society people are insisting on their rights without assuming their responsibilities. Consequently, marriages are failing, the country faces insoluble economic problems, social orders are disintegrating and human life is being sacrificed on altars of convenience.

Tragically, this inordinate concern for rights has invaded Christianity and the Church. Notice how much more is being said these days in Christian circles about what God must do for us than about what we must do for Him. Many Christians these days feel strongly that the church must meet their needs, but they do not have a corresponding awareness that they must serve the church.

This is a reflection of spiritual immaturity. Children expect to be catered to without having to pay for what they receive. And baby Christians want to be blessed and benefitted without having to sacrifice any personal interests for the sake of others or the Lord.

This emphasis on rights and the abrogation of responsibility also represents a great distance from the spirit of the Christ, whom we are supposed to be following. Jesus never worried about how He was treated, nor was He concerned about how He would be benefitted. He utterly gave Himself to the needs of others and to the interests of His Father's Kingdom.

The New Testament pictures the Kingdom of God advancing against error, dispelling darkness, overthrowing satanic strongholds and spreading the glory of God throughout the earth. And we are the soldiers through whom the Kingdom's cause must be advanced. But many of us are taken up with the size of our pay, the cut of our uniforms, the thickness of the mattresses upon which we sleep and the availability of recreational equipment. We have no heart for the trenches, the blood, sweat and tears of real warfare.

In a day that needs strong churches as never before, congregations are rent by people determined that things shall be done "their way." More and more church resources must be spent on keeping parishioners happy and comfortable. An epidemic of church conflicts is spreading across evangelicalism in North America.

In this matter, Christians must be entirely divorced from the spirit of this present age. Dr. A. B. Simpson wrote, "Here lies the great difference between the world's gospel and the Lord's Gospel. The world says, 'Take care of yourself.' The Lord says, 'Let yourself go, and take care of others and the glory of your God'" (*The Christ Life*, p. 83).

We need not concern ourselves at all about our rights. Instead, we need to assume responsibility: for the evangelization of the lost, for the care of the helpless and hurting, for the well-being of the Church, for the spiritual health of fellow believers, for the honor of God among men. When it comes to rights or responsibilities, there is no question where the Christian's priorities must be placed.

Activism without Holiness

Fran Sciacca, an author of several books and articles related to youth ministries, said once at a seminar, "Many believers today are substituting Christian activism for sanctified living." That assertion deserves our serious consideration.

This is an age of activism. Christian youth gather at school flagpoles to pray, thousands march for Jesus in major cities around the world, believers picket abortion clinics and line street corners holding signs that plead for the lives of the yet unborn. We are invited to give our allegiance to numerous causes—housing the homeless, staffing crisis pregnancy centers, opposing pornography, seeking to restore prayer to public schools. Increasingly, Christians are writing to legislators, petitioning school boards and appearing at city council meetings to make their views known.

To actively support just causes is not wrong. Clearly, some activism is necessary, especially when the society around us is plagued by such widespread moral deterioration.

The crucial word in Sciacca's statement, however, is "substituting." We can become so involved in the support of a cause or causes that we neglect the cultivation of personal holiness. We can be so concerned about moral issues that we neglect righteousness.

The actions of those who have attempted to kill abortion providers are an example of such substitution. They have been activists in a just cause—opposing abortion. But attempting to kill another person clearly is not consistent with sanctified living.

Attempting to murder abortion providers obviously is an extreme form of the condition Sciacca's comment describes. But such substitution can happen in lesser ways. Sometimes those who support just causes do so with arrogance, intolerance and vituperation. Sometimes individuals who are aggressive exponents of prayer in school do little praying in their own homes.

Some persons who vigorously support the maintenance of traditional family values manifest little of the spirit of Christ within their own homes. People who staunchly campaign against pornography can be troublemakers in their local church.

I am not trying to discourage activism. But I urge us to take inventory of our priorities. The New Testament puts far more emphasis upon personal holiness than upon support for just causes. God is more concerned about what we *are* than He is with what we *do*. The Bible does not tell God's people to clothe themselves with pro-life T-shirts but to put on "compassion, kindness, humility, gentleness and patience" (Colossians 3:12).

Jesus said that His followers were to be salt in the earth. But He also said that salt that had lost its saltiness was good for nothing (Matthew 5:13).

It is personal holiness that makes a Christian salty. Integrity, graciousness, love, purity—these are the qualities that must be in our lives if we are going to impact our world positively. Activism without personal holiness is ineffectual.

Peter's first epistle was written to people who lived in a world filled with immorality, injustice and corruption. In fact, Christians at that time were undergoing severe persecution. His advice is very instructive. "Live such good lives among the pagans," Peter wrote, "that, though they accuse you of doing wrong, they may see your good deeds and glorify God on the day he visits us" (1 Peter 2:12).

With all our marching, protesting, organizing for action and giving to causes, let us never forget that above all else God has called us to be holy people, filled with the fruit of the Spirit and conformed to the image of Christ.

Whose Fault
Is It?

In 1992, secular writer Charles J. Sykes published a book called *A Nation of Victims*. It is a very readable look at the tendency of people to excuse their failures and to absolve themselves of responsibility for their wrongs. Sykes writes,

> *American life is increasingly characterized by the plaintive insistence, I am a victim. . . . From the addicts of the South Bronx to the self-styled emotional road-kills of Manhattan's Upper East Side, the mantra of the victims is the same: I am not responsible; it's not my fault.*

Sykes goes on to say,

> *The ethos of victimization has an endless capacity . . . for exculpating one's self from blame, washing away responsibility in a torrent of explanations—racism, sexism, rotten parents, addiction and illness.*

Some recent court decisions support Sykes' thesis. Juries have excused murder, mayhem and mutilation on the grounds of extenuating circumstances.

This tendency to absolve ourselves from blame has affected religious life. Repentance is foundational to any genuine religious experience. Jesus said, "Unless you repent, you too will all perish" (Luke 13:3). We must come to God in humility and contrition. The psalmist wrote, "The sacrifices of God are a broken spirit; / a broken and contrite heart, / O God, you will not despise." (51:17)

But if a person does not feel responsible for his actions, he has nothing for which to repent. If he can transfer blame to some extenuating circumstance, he has no reason to be contrite. This is perhaps why today one seldom sees anyone weeping before God or demonstrating in some other way genuine sorrow for sin.

About all this, however, we must not be deceived. Before God we *are* responsible for our actions, and we *are* guilty for our sins. We must acknowledge the truth presented by Romans, chapters 1–3. "Men are without excuse" (1:20); "God 'will give to each person according to what he has done'" (2:6); "Jews and Gentiles alike are all under sin" (3:9).

People can rationalize their transgressions. Our tendencies *are* affected by what has happened in the past. We *are* more openly subjected to temptations than others have been in other generations. Satan *does* deceive. People around us *do* provoke us. In fact each of us has a fallen, depraved nature that we inherited from Adam. According to the attitude described by Charles Sykes in his book, we ought to try to roll all blame for actions over onto Adam. Or perhaps we should try to blame God Himself for allowing man to fall.

However, we are responsible for what we are and what we do because we can be delivered from wrongs and failures. A sudden lurch of the boat and a slippery deck may cause me to fall overboard into the ocean. But if someone throws me a life preserver and I refuse to grab it and therefore drown, I have no one but myself to blame. The Bible teaches that if we accept the light of nature and conscience and pursue righteousness, we will be led to deliverance. Finally, we will be brought by God to a Savior who can cleanse us from sin and change us into good people. If we do not accept this "lifeline" from God, we will fall under judgment with no one but ourselves to blame.

We must stop making excuses. Sykes says,

> *Defendants charged with murder, rape, and robbery have cited PMS, alcoholism, drug use, junk food, excessive television watching, and "lovesickness" in their defense. Mothers who kill their infant children have claimed that they suffered from postpartum depression.*

But God is not fooled by our rationalizations. He has offered us forgiveness, redemption and deliverance through His Son. If we continue in sin we have no one but ourselves to blame.

Who Is the Greatest among Us?

I admire individuals who can step down from positions of leadership gracefully.

No doubt at first most of those who aspire to hold some office in a local church or to be a denominational official desire only to do as much as possible for the Lord and welcome a larger sphere of service in order to accomplish more for Him. But subtly, without realizing it, some begin to enjoy the power and prestige that goes with position.

We naturally like to be in control. We are flattered by honors paid to us. We enjoy being the one who makes decisions rather than having to abide by what someone else decrees. We like being the boss. Consequently, sometimes presidents of organizations, district superintendents, field directors, elders or treasurers or Sunday school superintendents in a local church and the like who find their leadership being challenged begin to work at holding onto their positions, and some who are removed from office are deeply hurt. They feel demoted, abused, wronged.

Such people generally think they have good reasons for acting and feeling as they do. We can come up with all kinds of rationalizations for wanting to stay in office. But in fact we are never more worldly than when we grasp for position and when we strive to remain in places of prestige and power. In fact, we are conducting ourselves in an utterly unChristlike manner.

In Luke 22:25–26 Jesus said to His disciples, "The kings of the Gentiles lord it over them; and those who exercise authority over them call themselves Benefactors. *But you are not to be like that*" (emphasis mine). Jesus completely turned the tables on the world's ideas in this matter. He said, "The greatest among you should be like the youngest, and the one who rules like the one who serves" (Luke 22:26). Then Jesus set before us the standard by which we should conduct ourselves in this matter of leadership. He said, "For who is greater, the one who is at the table or

39

the one who serves? Is it not the one who is at the table? *But I am among you as one who serves*" (Luke 22:27, emphasis mine).

By Christ's example and by Christian principles, to leave a position of leadership is not to step down but to step up. To become a follower rather than a leader is not demotion but promotion. To be a servant rather than a master is not to be less but to be more. Jesus said, "The greatest among you will be your servant. For whoever exalts himself will be humbled, and whoever humbles himself will be exalted" (Matthew 23:11-12). And we must form our opinions and attitudes about leadership from Christ, not from the world. It is carnal pride, not the Word of God, that makes anyone delight in being in charge and seek to stay on top. It is worldly thinking that causes us to take pride in being in some "high" office.

Obviously some people must assume leadership roles. Every organization must have a head. Every church must have officers. God clearly calls certain individuals to positions of headship. First Timothy 3:1 says, "If anyone sets his heart on being an overseer, he desires a noble task."

But let no Christian flatter himself with the notion that this makes him better than others around him. Let none of us think of ourselves as great because of a position we hold. And if we are asked by the Lord to serve in some leadership role, let us never, never strive to hold onto our office or position. Rather let us be ready to step up in good grace to some other thing God has for us to do. Let us thank God if He honors us by calling us to the greater place of what by the world's standards is a lesser job.

If you are hurt or bitter because you were not reelected to some office, please listen to Jesus: "If anyone wants to be first, he must be the very last, and the servant of all" (Mark 9:35). If you have been struggling to hold onto a position that may be taken from you, remember that the Savior we serve girded Himself and got down and washed His disciples' feet.

Whose Money Is It?

One day several years ago I was having lunch with a success-ful Christian businessman. At the conclusion of the meal, as we quibbled over who would pay the check, I said, somewhat facetiously, "You should let me pay. You ought to save your money."

I have never forgotten his reply. He said, "I don't have any money. It all belongs to the Lord."

Since that day I have become increasingly convinced that what that man said about his money is the New Testament standard for every Christian. We talk about full consecration. We sing "All for Jesus, all for Jesus!" We remember that we are called by Romans 12:1 to present ourselves to God as living sacrifices.

That means that not 10 percent nor 15 percent of our wealth is God's but *all*, entirely all. We simply are entrusted with the management of His resources.

But what does proper stewardship of God's money entail? What percent of my income should I give to the church? Is it all right to have a savings account? Can a Christian own a boat? Should I buy a VCR? If we take seriously the truth that all our wealth belongs to the Lord, we are bound to ask such questions.

Fortunately, the Scripture gives us a lot of instruction in this matter. Philip Yancey, in a 1984 article in *Christianity Today*, says that over 450 separate biblical passages deal with the subject of money. Jesus spoke more often about money than about heaven or hell.

It is not my purpose now to try to survey all the teaching of God's Word about how we ought to use what He entrusts into our care. Rather, I want to urge us to search out and openheart-edly examine what God has told us in Scripture. There is, in my judgment, an enormous disparity between what God's Word teaches on this matter and how professed, Bible-believing Christians live.

I do want, however, to point out two broad principles that emerge strongly out of all the Bible says about financial matters. The first is this: We are not to pursue money in order to possess it and its advantages for ourselves and our families.

Thousands of Christians avidly strive for additional wealth in order to add to their store of possessions, to gain prestige, to make their lives more comfortable and to be able to afford more pleasurable activities. But what could be clearer than Christ's words in Matthew 6:19, "Do not store up for yourselves treasures on earth"?

Paul told Timothy to flee from a desire for money. He said, "People who want to get rich fall into temptation and a trap and into many foolish and harmful desires that plunge men into ruin and destruction" (1 Timothy 6:9). Paul further warned, "For the love of money is a root of all kinds of evil" (6:10). Jesus said, "You cannot serve both God and Money" (Matthew 6:24). Plainly, the Bible teaches that we are not to want money for its advantages to us.

The other broad principle is this: When we have money, we should give away as much as possible.

Why should a person work? Ephesians 4:28 answers, "that he may have something to share with those in need." Why does God prosper His children? Second Corinthians 9:11 says, "so that you can be generous on every occasion." Philip Yancey writes, "We can disarm the power of money . . . by giving it away."

Giving ennobles us and brings joy to our hearts. Giving affords us an opportunity to demonstrate our faith in God's ability to care for us. (See Matthew 6:25–34.) Giving provides us an opportunity to express gratitude and praise to God. The great value of money lies not in our ability to possess it, spend it or use it but to give it away.

I am aware that this is different from how most of us approach money. But we claim to be Bible-believing Christians. I urge us to let the teachings of Scripture control this area of our lives.

An Audit of
Our Giving

Most North Americans keep a record of their charitable contributions in order to claim these as deductions. Thus, their annual income tax returns become an audit of their giving. I wonder how many Christians have looked at their most recent figures and have been confronted with the fact that they gave less than 10 percent of their income to the Lord's work.

That 10 percent standard for giving comes from the biblical emphasis on tithing. Under Old Testament Law, people were required to bring a tithe (the word means 10 percent) of all they received to the temple and to present this as an offering to God. I have heard some Bible teachers argue that various offerings and sacrifices required by the Law, in addition to the tithe, raised the Old Testament level of required giving to 15 to 17 percent. In any case, the tithe (10 percent) was the basic Old Testament requirement.

Most Christians and Christian churches believe that this 10 percent standard carries over into the New Testament and that the tithe is the minimum amount any believer ought to give to the Lord today. Most pastors will preach on giving at least once or twice a year, and they will declare the tithe to be a standard for Christian stewardship.

Some Christians argue that New Testament Christians are not bound to tithe since we are under grace, not law. They object to an emphasis on tithing as being a legalistic practice inconsistent with the freedom we enjoy in Christ. Still, those who take this view must ask themselves if a New Testament believer's response with his resources should be anything less than an Old Testament person gave to God.

Generally, among Christians, the tithe is a recognized standard for giving to the Lord's work. But then those of us who live in the United States and Canada fill out our annual tax returns, and those forms audit our giving. And a lot of Christians would be embarrassed if their level of charitable contributions was made public. Statistics indicate that many Christians give less than 10 percent of their income to the Lord.

In some cases this may be an indication of a low level of devotion. Inevitably, what we do with our money is a reflection of our heart interests. If we love God fervently, we will give to His work generously and joyfully. But the plain truth is that some of us do not meet the standard of the tithe because our hearts are set on other things instead of on our Lord.

In some instances a failure to tithe results from a lack of faith. Admittedly we find it difficult, when money is scarce, to set aside at least 10 percent for the Lord first. At the beginning of the week or at the first of the month, we may have $115 worth of bills for every $100 we have received in income. How can we give $10 of each $100 to the Lord? We must at this point dare to believe the Word of God. The Lord has promised to supply the needs of those who give to Him, and millions of people have proved God generous in this regard. Somehow, when we give the Lord His part first, $90 goes further than $100.

Some people's failure to tithe is the result of carelessness. They have every intention to honor the Lord. However, they fail systematically to set aside God's portion first. Instead they wait until confronted by some special appeal or they tell themselves they will give more at some later time. Then when they look for money to contribute, nothing is left in the checking account. Impulse giving almost never measures up to the 10 percent standard.

Filling out the annual forms and paying income taxes is painful for most North Americans. But it can be a valuable experience if that audit wakes us up to our failure and causes us to give more generously.

Parents with
Wayward Children

Some Christian parents have been placed under a burden of guilt they should not have to bear. These parents have done a good job rearing their children. They have taken them to Sunday school and church services. They have urged them to accept Christ as their personal Savior.

But these parents have children who, in their late teens or in adulthood, have drifted away from the church or rebelled against the Lordship of Christ over their lives. Some may have sons or daughters who are far from God and into drugs, drinking or divorce.

Many evangelical Christians today seem convinced that if children have strayed from the Lord, their parents must have done something wrong or failed to rear their children properly. In an editorial in the May 13, 1992, issue of *Alliance Life*, I referred to a book that denigrates Dr. A. W. Tozer, a well-known writer, preacher and former editor of this magazine, because, allegedly, his children did not turn out well.

His information about Tozer's children, as it happens, was false. But the author who made these assertions obviously came to his conclusions on the assumption that if children go wrong they must have had poor fathers and/or mothers. He obviously believes parents bear full responsibility for all their children's later behavior.

Modern psychology has contributed to this perception. Many psychologists claim that all abnormal behavior and emotional difficulties can be traced to a person's childhood. Thus, practitioners search a man or woman's early years for some failure by their parents, and the responsibility for their client's problems then is loaded onto his or her mom or dad. And this concept now is taught in behavioral science classes. It even has been used to defend the actions of criminals.

As a result, some Christian parents who have wayward children are made to assume all responsibility for how their off-spring are living. They often are reluctant to discuss their children's problems because they know they will be demeaning themselves in the eyes of their Christian peers. Some have been told to their faces by fellow Christians that they must have been poor parents. In some cases children openly blame their parents for their difficulties.

This is not right. Obviously, parents have a great deal to do with how their children develop. Unquestionably, how parents rear their children more than any other thing determines their future behavior.

Still, every child is a free moral agent with his own mind and will. Ultimately, he is responsible for his own actions. Parents can do everything right and still have children who do wrong.

Proverbs 22:6 says, "Train a child in the way he should go, and when he is old he will not turn from it." But Proverbs also acknowledges that a son may not heed his father's teaching (13:1). Elsewhere in Proverbs, we read that a child may despise his mother (15:20), that he may mock his father and scorn obedience (30:17), and that he may even curse his parents (30:11, 20:20). And most important, Proverbs teaches that ultimately it is a child's own responsibility to accept and live by what he is taught by good parents (2:1–5). A properly reared child never can escape the *training* he has received. But he can, as a free moral agent, turn aside from the *ways* of righteousness.

Christian parents of children who have gone astray weep over their offspring. They agonize about the unrighteousness and neglect of God they see in their sons and daughters. They do not need the added burden of accepting blame for their children's waywardness. And those of us who have good kids dare not feel any pride in our parenthood. Without the grace of God, our children, too, may have gone astray.

Whatever Happened to Discipline?

The Scriptures tell us little about the childhood of Jesus. All the inspired information available to us is contained in just 13 verses in Luke 2.

Still, these verses provide some valuable insights into an ideal family life, and one statement in Luke is particularly significant in light of what goes on in many North American homes today.

Luke 2:51 says Jesus was obedient to His parents. That means Mary and Joseph exercised authority within their home, and Jesus submitted to their discipline.

That kind of a home prepares a child to live in a world where he must submit to other kinds of authority, such as that of teachers, government officials and employers. It lays the groundwork for a proper appreciation for and response to the government of God.

Such a home provides needed parental direction and regulation. Children simply do not possess sufficient intelligence and experience to make wise choices when left on their own.

Child psychologists have discovered that children who live in homes with clearly defined regulations, limits and punishments for violations of rules feel more secure. Some may rebel, but down deep they appreciate being told what to do and what is prohibited.

Despite this, parental authority and discipline is disappearing from many North American households. I have heard mothers say, "We never say 'no' to our children." I have seen mothers and fathers who have virtually no control over their offspring. I recently observed on an airplane a mother struggling with a child who had her totally intimidated and utterly exasperated.

Partly, this lack of parental control over children stems from books on child care. Some so-called modern authorities on child rearing tell young parents that rules inhibit a child's psychological development. They are told that saying "no" to a child frustrates his sense of self-worth.

Such instruction is wrong. Obviously, over-restriction and oppressive regulation can be harmful. But God sought to establish order and bring good to society by giving us laws and prescribing punishments for the violation of those laws. And the same principles apply to family life. Parents must determine what is acceptable behavior for their children and enforce it.

Often, parental control also is undermined when both mother and father are employed outside the home. Parents, especially mothers, who have been away all day at an office, store or classroom may feel guilty for not being at home more. Thus they cannot bring themselves to impose restrictions upon or apply discipline to their kids. And they are usually tired and therefore take the line of least resistance and give in to their children's behavior.

Unfortunately, children quickly learn to exploit this situation, and they become all the more demanding and undisciplined. Frustrated parents then buy more and more toys to pacify their children, or they encourage the youngsters to watch videos to quiet them, neither of which is a wholesome, constructive form of parenting.

Some parents simply lack the will to expend the effort to control their children. The proper exercise of parental authority takes time because children need to understand the rules to which they are subjected.

Discipline must be maintained with consistency. Parents cannot be severe one day and oblivious to disobedience the next. Punishment brings pain to the mother or father as well as to the child. To apply discipline properly, parents must understand their children's behavior and follow up on the discipline's effect.

It is easier, then, to ignore the matter of discipline and hope for the best. But this is not an option for Christian parents. Luke 2:51 shows us that we are required by God to establish parental authority in the home and see that our children learn obedience.

If there ever was an area in which Christians should be different from the world, it is in the quality of family life. We should take Christ's home as our example.

Christians
Must Read

A mong people in North America who consider themselves to be Christians there is a striking degree of ignorance concerning the Bible. Studies conducted by the Barna Research group found that of people who have Bibles in their homes, 58 percent did not know who preached the Sermon on the Mount. (A significant number answered "Billy Graham.") Half of those surveyed could not name the four Gospels. Half answered that the "Book of Thomas" was a part of Scripture, but they were not sure if it was in the Old or New Testament.

Along with such biblical ignorance there is among present-day Christians a corresponding lack of theological understanding. Many churchgoing people cannot define or support from Scripture such basic doctrinal concepts as the universal sinfulness of man, the deity of Christ, justification by faith or sanctification. At a dinner I once attended for a group of Christians of the community where I lived, someone at my table began to speak of a new work of the Holy Spirit in her life. A pastor's wife sitting next to her said, "What is the Holy Spirit?"

Such deficiency of understanding is serious. It is responsible for superficial Christian experience. It contributes to a lack of discernment, leaving people vulnerable to deception and error. If God's Word is spiritual meat and Christians are not ingesting and digesting that Word, the whole Body of Christ will be anemic, prone to disease and powerless for service.

Unless something is done, this dearth of biblical and theological knowledge will worsen. Generally, people are attending fewer church services than before (where, presumably, biblical and theological understanding is communicated through preaching). Most people will tolerate sermons no longer than 30 minutes. Fewer adults attend Sunday school classes. And fewer Christians are reading and studying on their own initiative.

All this leads me to suggest that local churches must encourage reading. We must rekindle in people an interest in the Bible itself and in good magazines and books. If they are not going to learn from sermons and Sunday school classes, people desperately need that additional knowledge and refined understanding that good reading matter will bring to their lives.

Churches may have to begin with literacy classes. There are somewhere between 30 and 60 million people in the United States who are functionally illiterate. Men and women will never profit from the good teaching of books and magazines if they cannot read. They may have to be taught how.

Children in Sunday school and in church-conducted club programs must be encouraged toward Christian literature. A few years ago a great many churches established libraries. But in many places those books are hardly touched today. Planned programs of reading ought to be built into Sunday school curriculums and club programs with awards for achievements. Leaders should talk about books, actually have them in hand and introduce the content of certain volumes.

I remember as a boy being urged by a Sunday school teacher to read missionary biographies. Those stories made a lasting impact upon me. I wonder how many church youth of this age have ever heard of Hudson Taylor, John G. Paton, David Livingston or Mary Slessor.

Church leaders should make books and magazines available to adults. Churches ought to maintain a book room or book table. The pastor should recommend certain articles or particular volumes and have those recommended magazines or books on hand for sale. The church in which I grew up always had a book table, with deeper-life and missionary volumes on sale, at every annual missions conference. Much of my early Christian reading material came from that table.

Fewer and fewer people are reading, and serious personal study is becoming increasingly rare. And the church is suffering as a result. This unfortunate trend cannot easily be reversed, but we must try. Ignorance is not bliss. It is a cause of spiritual anemia that cannot help but lead to an increasingly impotent and diseased church.

A Forgotten
Commandment

Most Christians—and Jews—would agree that the Ten Commandments provide a necessary foundation for moral order among human beings. People must not murder each other. Adultery is wrong. Individuals must not lie nor steal.

Those who violate these laws hurt themselves and others. The society that fails to maintain these standards imperils its existence.

This is true with respect to each commandment, including one that receives little emphasis today. Exodus 20:8 says, "Remember the Sabbath day by keeping it holy."

A professional football player once justified to me his participation in games on Sunday by saying, "A person is not saved by keeping the law." I quite agree. I am not, however, discussing what one must do to be saved. Rather I am concerned about our living life as God says it ought to be lived. And I am concerned about the effect our conduct has on the social order of which we are a part.

God laid down as a basic law that one day in seven should be different from the rest. The Jews set Saturday apart as that day. Christians generally recognize Sunday as that special, seventh day.

That day is to be holy. "Holy," in its simplest sense, means set apart to belong to the Lord. Therefore, the seventh day is to be a day set apart as belonging especially to God.

Our standard with respect to the seventh day's use must not be what is good for me or what I enjoy but what is good for God and what pleases Him. It is not a period in the week designed primarily for our respite and recreation. It is much more clearly a day for a cessation of other pursuits in order to have time to seek the Lord and to know Him better.

God has made this law for *our* benefit and for the benefit of the society of which we are a part.

51

We need a day each week during which we concentrate upon the Lord. The knowledge of God is the source of eternal life. Fellowship with God is the richest privilege afforded to man. The worship of God is life's loftiest vocation. The help of God is our most precious resource. Yet all influences of the physical world around us dim our vision of the Lord. The daily demands we face distract us from intimacy with Him. Responsibilities related to work, education and family easily can take all our waking hours. Our inescapable need for sleep, rest and recreation consume our hours.

Without a special day set aside for God, a day in which we set aside other things to seek Him, we are likely to miss Him completely. Thus we can be robbed of our greatest treasure: an increasingly vital union with our Creator and Father.

In addition, our world needs the testimony to God's importance that is provided by our giving honor to God one day in seven.

Proverbs 29:18 says, "Where there is no vision, the people perish" (KJV). This verse says that without a consciousness of God a people will start to disintegrate. The New International Version says, "Where there is no revelation, the people cast off restraint." When people lose sight of God they become lawless. Morality is undermined. Forces of disintegration begin to tear apart society from within.

Those of us who know God have a responsibility to honor Him among men and to do so conspicuously, so as to remind people of His existence and to call them to a consideration of their accountability to Him. When we give God one day in seven we say to the world that God still reigns. We testify that He is still a factor to be reckoned with and a Person to be considered.

Many Christians have abused what we believe to be our liberty in Christ. We think ourselves entitled to do just about anything we please on the Lord's Day—sleep, play, travel, buy, sell and work. But we ignore God's law to our own loss and harm. And we contribute to the growing secularism that is drawing society toward its destruction. Our misuse of the seventh day is serious.

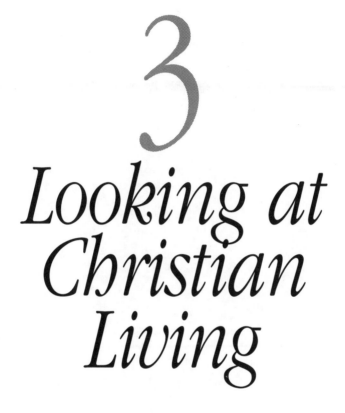

3
Looking at Christian Living

Something Better
Than Blessings

It is proper for a Christian to be grateful to God for the blessings He bestows upon us. A gospel song admonishes us to name our blessings one by one.

Most of our testimonies focus on the good things God has given us in Christ. We thank the Lord for His healing touch, for supplying our financial needs, for giving us peace and joy and hope. And we should. Psalm 103:2 tells us to "forget not all His benefits."

A great deal of the teaching we receive from pulpits and from the Christian press also reminds us of the good things God pours out upon those who belong to Him. We are told He wants to prosper us, heal all our diseases and satisfy our mouths with good things. And there are scriptural bases for such promises. Psalm 84:11 says, "no good thing does he withhold / from those whose walk is blameless."

Still, we should recognize that there is something better for the believer than God's blessings. That is the knowledge of and fellowship with God Himself.

Great saints of the past sought after God rather than for His benefits. Fredrick Faber spoke to his own heart:

Oh then wish more for God, burn more with desire,
Covet more the dear sight of His marvelous face.

Charles Wesley wrote:

Thou Shepherd of Israel, and mine,
The joy and desire of my heart,
For closer communion I pine;
I long to reside where Thou art.

The psalmist was not asking for things from God but for God Himself when he said in Psalm 42:1–2:

As the deer pants for streams of water,
  so my soul pants for you, O God.
My soul thirsts for God, for the living God.

The heart aspiration of the apostle Paul was expressed not in a prayer for material prosperity or for peace and happiness. Rather he proclaimed, "I want to know Christ" (Philippians 3:10).

These writers understood that God Himself is a greater treasure than any blessing He can bestow. Communion with Him is far more satisfying than riches He may extend to us or benefits He might provide. God Himself is enough. When we see His glory, rest in His presence, bathe our souls in the light of His radiance, discover the treasures of His wisdom and revel in the consciousness of His love, other things pale into insignificance.

Actually, God's blessing can cause us to miss the Lord Himself. A businessman came back from a trip away from home eager to spend some time with his young son. But he found his son so taken up with a new toy he had brought him that the boy had no time for his dad.

Sometimes we can be so taken up with God's gifts to us that we have little time for the Lord Himself. Often it is those who have lost all their material possessions, those who have gone through personal privation and suffering, who seem to know the greater riches of deep communion with God.

Upon what do we have our hearts set? For what do we pray? There is something better than God's blessings. We should long for God Himself.

Albert B. Simpson put it this way in the hymn entitled "Himself":

Once it was the blessing,
  Now it is the Lord;
Once it was the feeling,
  Now it is His Word;
Once His gift I wanted,
  Now the Giver own;
Once I sought for healing,
  Now Himself alone.

Transcending
Trivialities

A novel I was reading some time ago described the theft of a valuable painting from a heavily guarded gallery in Europe. The thieves succeeded in stealing the piece of art by using a simple device.

An art student, with his easel, paint and brushes, was copying another picture in the room where the painting to be stolen was located. A young woman, an accomplice of the robbers, tripped over the easel, knocking it down and spilling the copyist's paints as she fell to the floor.

The guards rushed over to help the young woman to her feet, to set the easel upright again and to clean up the spilled paints. While the guards were thus distracted, the thieves cut the picture they were after out of its frame, secreted it beneath clothing and hurried from the building before the loss of the art treasure was discovered.

Not long ago I read of a freak auto accident. A man, driving alone down a highway, noticed crumbs on his shirt left there from his lunch. While brushing these crumbs away, his attention was distracted from the road. When he looked up again he was in a curve that he failed to negotiate. And the car flipped over into a ditch.

It seems to me that in a similar way the church is often victimized by distractions that take its focus away from those issues upon which the concerns and energies of believers should be concentrated. We often seem to be absorbed with trivialities while we neglect major matters.

For example, some individuals distribute literature and buttonhole fellow believers and provoke discussions in Sunday school classes in order to denounce the observance of Halloween by Christians. (Halloween has pagan origins and occult associations.) However, these same individuals do not demonstrate a corresponding degree of concern about praying and encouraging others to pray for the millions in our world who are still without Christ.

I once visited a church almost torn apart by disagreement over whether a kitchen ought to be included in the new building the congregation was erecting. I did not hear any discussion that weekend about strategies to reach the unchurched in the neighborhood where the new building was being located.

I remember a meeting in which many of those attending completely forgot that they had come to worship Almighty God and to seek His face. They were upset because they felt the person who was leading the meeting was dressed inappropriately.

This is not to suggest that Christians should not have convictions about holidays and proper conduct in church buildings and appropriate dress. I am not saying such issues ought never to be raised. However, I am persuaded that we can be distracted from more important matters by giving too much attention to relatively trivial things.

That statement, of course, raises the question of how one is to decide what is trivial and what is not. Everyone tends to think his or her concerns are of supreme importance. But surely Christians can agree that certain things really do matter.

Sincere worship to Almighty God, the exaltation of Jesus Christ, the evangelization of the lost who are around us, the spread of the gospel to every yet unreached people group, relief for those in our world who are suffering—these are the kinds of larger issues upon which we should focus.

We must not allow ourselves to be all taken up with causes that have little eternal significance. We must not expend valuable time and energy on matters that mean little in terms of the building of God's Kingdom. We ought not to waste resources and emotion on petty disputes when we have yet so much of the Great Commission to fulfill.

To keep God's work from being accomplished Satan does not have to kill off Christian believers. He need only distract them with a concern about trivialities.

Loving Christ,
Again

The brochure advertised a conference to be held on the East Coast of the United States. Since I knew immediately I would not be able to attend, I laid the brochure aside. However, one phrase from the description of the purpose of the conference remained imprinted upon my mind: "Fall in love with Jesus—all over again!"

Those words reminded me that love for Jesus Christ is the essence of genuine Christian spirituality. One cannot miss the New Testament emphasis upon the importance of loving Christ. Jesus said, "If God were your Father, you would love me" (John 8:42). Again, He said, "He who loves me will be loved by my Father" (John 14:21).

After His Resurrection from the dead, Christ probed the nature of Peter's discipleship with the searching question, "Simon son of John, do you truly love me?" (21:16). Second Corinthians 5:14 speaks of being constrained by the love of Christ (KJV). First Peter 1:8 speaks of loving Him even though we have not seen Him personally.

A personal passion for Christ has characterized the lives of the sweetest saints, the most heroic martyrs and the Church's most devoted servants. It is love for Jesus Christ that gives wings to worship, puts zeal into Christian work and motivates holy living.

That phrase "Fall in love with Jesus—all over again!", however, points to the real possibility in Christian experience of a waning devotion to Christ. We remember the condemnation of the Ephesian congregation in Revelation 2:4, "Yet I hold this against you: You have forsaken your first love." And we must confess that evidence of deep affection for Jesus often is missing from the lives of evangelical Christians today.

We are involved in all kinds of religious activities. We quibble about ecclesiastical forms and procedures. We worry about moral deterioration and declining Christian influence in society.

And too often these things crowd out a concern about our individual relationship with Jesus Christ Himself.

As our Savior moved among people preoccupied with religious appearances, personal aggrandizement and political freedom, He kept trying to focus their attention upon the essential matter of man's love for God. And the Holy Spirit today seeks to bring Christians to the supreme matter of love for Jesus Christ.

Actually, one does not "fall in love" with Jesus. The kind of love about which the New Testament speaks is not merely a sentimental attraction to Jesus. We must choose to love Him.

To love Jesus as we ought, we also must give time to Him— to a contemplation of His person, to communion with Him, to a saturation of our souls with His presence.

One of the most poignant pictures in the New Testament is suggested by Revelation 3:20. The resurrected, living, glorious Christ stands outside the door of a church, knocking so as to enter and to sit down to supper. But He remains outside.

I am afraid it is a situation altogether too common today. Christ is outside, denied a central place in our interests, time and affections.

Frederick Faber wrote:

O, Jesus, Jesus, dearest Lord!
Forgive me if I say;
For very love, Thy sacred name
A thousand times a day.

The second verse of that hymn reads,

I love Thee so I know not how
My transports to control;
Thy love is like a burning fire,
Within my very soul.

That song represents a level of devotion to Jesus Christ far above mine. However, I want to love Jesus Christ like that. And I long to see more of that kind of personal adoration for Jesus Christ expressed in the lives of my fellow believers. What a difference that would make in today's church!

It Costs to Serve
the Lord

Several years ago I participated in a 10-day conference in Hong Kong. Dr. Philip Teng was the main speaker. At one service, just before he preached, the conference music director led the 2,000 or so people in the congregation in singing a chorus that proclaimed, "It pays to serve Jesus." When Dr. Teng got up to speak, his first words were, "My friends, it does not *pay* to serve Jesus. It *costs* to serve Him."

I think of that incident when I watch ministers try to attract people to Christianity by pointing out the benefits of knowing Christ without also stating the demands of discipleship. I think of Dr. Teng's remarks when I read of churches that seek to grow by promising people prosperity and by making religion as comfortable as possible while ignoring all the New Testament says about sacrifice and suffering for Christ's sake.

None of us can contribute anything toward the cost of *providing* salvation. Jesus paid it all. By His death on the cross Christ fulfilled all the Law's demands and purchased our pardon. We are redeemed from sin, reconciled to God and made heirs of eternal life entirely by His work on our behalf.

But the good news of the availability of salvation in Jesus must be preached in all the nations of the earth. People everywhere must hear the gospel and be persuaded to trust in the Savior. And this is a program in which every Christian is to be involved. All of us are called to participate in some way in the propagation of the gospel among all people everywhere.

This is where the cost comes in. Philippians 1:29 says to believers, "For it has been granted to you on behalf of Christ not only to believe on him, but also to suffer for him." For Peter this meant being imprisoned, threatened and, ultimately (according to tradition), crucified. For Paul, his efforts to preach Christ everywhere meant being beaten, stoned, thrown into prison and suffering a shipwreck.

61

Across the centuries the blood of martyrs has been the seed of the Church. I own a copy of the book *Twenty-Five Wonderful Years*, a history of the first quarter-century of The Christian and Missionary Alliance. Fully one-third of the book is devoted to a list of people, with a brief paragraph about each one, who died in the service of the Lord under the Alliance. Most of those named in this section of the book laid down their lives in India, China and Africa. Some died within days or weeks after arriving on their fields. In those years the C&MA was a small denomination. Yet in its first 25 years, 145 of its missionaries died in the service of the Lord.

How can we imagine that it no longer takes blood, sweat and tears to penetrate the darkness of unevangelized areas and win people to Christ? How dare we think we should

Be carried to the skies
On flowery beds of ease
While others fight to win the prize
And sail through bloody seas?

Must we not hear our Lord calling us to sacrifice and suffering for His sake as He has called to His servants in every other generation?

I think as I write this of several young Alliance missionary women in their 30s who have died in the past two years. No one can say for sure that these women would not have died were they housewives in America or Canada. But I believe they were casualties of the spiritual war that God's soldiers are waging against the forces of sin, death and hell.

The fact is that it costs to get the gospel to people who have not yet been persuaded to receive Him. This work requires of God's people travailing prayer, sacrificial giving, exhausting work and, in some cases, even the laying down of lives. Any presentation of Christianity that ignores this truth is a distortion, a perversion.

When I think of the price others have paid to wholly follow the Lord, I must ask myself if I am carrying my share, bearing my part of the cost of proclaiming the gospel to those who must be saved. How about you?

The Pain
of Love

One of Frederick Faber's poems is entitled "The Pain of Love." That same expression was used by the character of C. S. Lewis in a drama that portrays the relationship between that noted English professor and author and his wife, Joy, whom he married late in life and who shortly thereafter died of cancer.

The phrase embodies profound truth. Genuine love inevitably does involve pain. Perhaps this is why we see so little authentic love in our world today.

Genuine love is the deliberate devotion of oneself to the happiness and fulfillment of another individual. It is a determination to seek the highest good of some other person.

This means setting aside our own desires and sacrificing our personal interests. It means doing what is best for someone else rather than what benefits us.

This may involve so simple an act as a mother feeding her hungry baby first when she herself is starving. It may mean passing up an outstanding career opportunity in order to help a spouse "make it" in his or her chosen profession.

Our selfish human natures smart at such sacrifices. Setting aside personal aims and gains for the sake of others hurts. Yet this is a delightful pain. One who truly loves finds great personal satisfaction in doing what benefits others.

Personal sacrifices are hard, however. And today selfishness is everywhere encouraged; self-seeking is a cardinal virtue. A man, we are told, must grab all he can for himself. A woman must strive for her "rights." Such an atmosphere leaves little room for the altruism of true love.

Love is painful, too, because we feel frustrated at our inabilities to do more and to demonstrate our affection more perfectly to the one to whom we are devoted. This, especially, was the cause of the anguish Faber felt in his poem. He wrote of love to Christ and described his disappointment with these words:

*The more I love thee, Lord, the more
I hate my own cold heart.*

Yet in this day we are encouraged to avoid any negative thoughts concerning ourselves. We are to feel good about ourselves, be proud of what we are. That mind-set, in turn, discourages us from becoming so committed to someone else that we risk disappointment in our failures toward that person. Hence fewer people today really love.

Because the one who loves is dedicated to seeking the highest and best for another, he hurts over every need and privation suffered by the object of his affection. Because C. S. Lewis allowed himself to love Joy, he agonized over the suffering that cancer brought into her life. Christ wept over His beloved Jerusalem because He knew that her rejection of Him would lead to her destruction.

This holds true even when one's love reaches out to embrace large groups of people. The person who chooses to love the world hurts over reports of starvation, injustice and oppression. He feels real anguish at the plight of those who are perishing without the knowledge of the saving truth of the gospel.

But Christians, we are told, should be perpetually happy. A smiling face, a cheerful spirit is a sure mark of genuine spirituality. We are to avoid anything sobering or gloomy.

Consequently, the very atmosphere of our day discourages love. We dare not care too much about others, lest we find ourselves weeping with those who weep. Better that we ignore the problems of society and the plight of the doomed lest our spirits be weighed down with sorrow.

The spirit of our day militates against genuine love. And love will become increasingly rare as long as selfishness and pride and frivolity are the order of the day.

However, if we avoid the pain of love we ultimately will experience a greater wound. Man finds his greatest fulfillment and satisfaction in loving God and loving others. If we refuse to love in order to avoid its pain, we consign ourselves to an emptiness of spirit that is far worse than the hurt love will bring.

When You Have Been Hurt

Twice recently, I have met or heard about people who no longer go to church because they were offended by something that was said or done to them by someone in the congregation with which they formerly were associated. "He was hurt, and he doesn't go anymore." "After the way she was treated, she quit attending." Across the years I have heard such comments perhaps two dozen times.

In many cases that kind of statement is, in reality, only an excuse, a cover for the real reasons for not attending. The heart of the offended individual already was cold toward the Lord. She already had lost interest in spiritual things. He may never have had a genuine hunger for God nor love for His Word. The slight or cutting remark simply provided a convenient rationale for ceasing association with church activities.

On the other hand, sometimes individuals who sincerely are interested and involved are mistreated or insulted or criticized unfairly. And I admit that it is difficult to worship and serve in a church, especially a small one, when you must do so alongside someone who has hurt you. This is especially true when the person who has offended you is a church leader.

But is staying away from the church the right response? Or do we actually compound the hurt to *ourselves* when we decide not to participate in church activities anymore?

Church services provide us an opportunity to worship the Lord, and worship is not an option but an obligation. We were created to worship the Lord. And we can engage in no more wholesome and uplifting activity than worship.

Some people argue that they can worship God at home or outdoors, but in fact they seldom really worship that way. We need the congregational singing, the praying together and the public proclamation of God's Word that takes place during church services.

65

If we stay away because we have been hurt or angered, we deny to God praise and honor that ought to be offered to Him. And we rob ourselves of the personally enriching experience of coming into God's presence with our thanksgiving and adoration.

Church activities provide needed fellowship with other believers. Christians pray for one another, encourage each other and provide help in times of need. This is why Hebrews 10:25 says, "Let us not give up meeting together." Despite the fact that some church people can be unkind, there are scores of others who are good, kind and generous. Why should we cut ourselves off from them? We need them and they need us.

Church activities provide teaching that is important to our spiritual development. The preaching, Sunday school classes, Bible studies—we need these to grow in grace and in the knowledge of the Lord. We can study the Scripture on our own. Christian programs on radio and television can be helpful. But there is no substitute for the preaching and teaching offered by a local church.

Staying away from church helps no one, solves nothing and only further damages our lives. What, then, should we do?

Ephesians 4:32 says, "Be kind and compassionate to one another, forgiving each other, just as in Christ God forgave you." Colossians 3:13 speaks even more specifically to the issue I have been discussing: "Bear with each other and forgive whatever grievances you may have against one another. Forgive as the Lord forgave you."

Our model is God's forgiveness. We offended God. We hurt Him deeply by our sins, by our neglect of Him, by our disobedience. Yet He completely forgives us. He does not remain offended. He does not cut Himself off from us.

We need the enabling of the Holy Spirit to do so, but we are to forgive those who have offended us and remain in fellowship with the church and as a participant in its activities.

Staying away from church hurts us. By God's grace we must forgive and go forward.

A Root of Bitterness

When I first met Clyde he was very antagonistic toward Christianity and not at all interested in going to church. I learned that earlier in his life he had been active in an evangelical congregation. However, something happened at that church that deeply offended him, and he became bitter.

For the next two years after becoming acquainted with him, I tried to befriend this man. From time to time we played golf together. During those two years I attempted, on several occasions but without success, to bring up the subject of his relationship with the Lord.

Then a crisis in his family disturbed him and opened his heart. When, at that time, I invited him to get right with the Lord, he responded. From that day until his death, Clyde was a faithful servant of the Lord.

One day, as we discussed his experience, Clyde told me that when he once again opened his life to Christ's saving grace, it was as if a veil was lifted within his mind. He said, "Spiritual truths that were utterly blacked out of my consciousness during those years when I was bitter came back to me. Joy and peace I had not felt for years returned." He said, "My anger and resentment had put me into spiritual darkness."

That man's experience is not unusual. Hebrews 12:15 warns us against allowing a root of bitterness to grow up within us, and bitterness in the human spirit can be disastrous. As it did to my friend, bitterness distorts our perspective, clouds our understanding and closes our hearts. And, as the metaphor in Hebrews 12:15 suggests, bitterness grows and grows until it crowds out virtue, peace and joy.

Some churches these days have within them individuals who constantly find fault, oppose change and stir up disputes. They think they are entirely right in their opinions, and they will not listen to any counsel or correction. Some of these people are blinded by bitterness. It affects their thinking whether they realize it or not.

Someone reading this may have been offended in the past. You were hurt by the actions of a fellow Christian, perhaps by a church or by a pastor. Those actions may have been totally unjust and unfair. You may feel you have a right to be bitter.

However, if you allow resentment to remain in your spirit, you, ultimately, will be the loser. That spirit will close your heart to grace and blind your mind to truth. For your own sake, you must forgive. You must forget the wrong and gain victory over the anger. Right now you may feel that you are totally justified in continuing to resent what happened, but if you feel that way this is proof that your perspective already has been distorted.

If possible, go to the individual or group of persons that did you wrong. Or write a letter. Say, "I completely forgive you with no reservations attached." Even though you were wronged, take the initiative to clear the air and resolve any differences that remain. Then ask God to cleanse your mind and soul of any bitterness that lingers there.

No wrong that was done, no hurt that you suffered can do you ultimate harm. It will not destroy your spiritual life unless you allow it to bring bitterness into your soul. I invite you, by God's grace, to triumph over that bitterness and find freedom and joy in a release from resentment. If there is anger in your heart, take it to Calvary and find release there by identifying yourself with the Savior who forgave those who nailed Him to a cross.

Greatness and
Hard Work

I am convinced that no person has achieved true greatness who did not put in long hours of hard work. Obviously, I do not know enough about every great person who has ever existed to prove my contention, but the lives of two great men from the past surely lend credibility to my thesis.

No one can question the greatness of John Wesley and Albert B. Simpson. They were godly men of enormous spiritual power. Each made a tremendous impact upon his age.

They also were untiring workers. For many years Wesley annually traveled, on average, 1,000 miles on horseback throughout the British isles. He seldom preached less than a thousand times a year. Additionally, Wesley administered the activities of a network of Methodist societies throughout England. The *New Schaff-Herzog Encyclopedia of Religious Knowledge* says in regard to Wesley:

> *He formed societies, opened chapels, examined and commissioned preachers, administered discipline, raised funds for schools, chapels, and charities, prescribed for the sick, superintended schools and orphanages, prepared commentaries and a vast amount of other religious literature, replied to attacks on Methodism, conducted controversies and carried on a prodigious correspondence.*

Simpson also produced an enormous amount of work. He regularly caught a 6:18 A.M. train from Nyack, New York, to New Jersey and then a ferry across the Hudson River to New York City. In the city he pastored a very busy church and administered the affairs of The Christian and Missionary Alliance.

At the same time, Simpson was writing for and editing a magazine, publishing books, composing hymns and traveling around the country to conferences and conventions. Simpson wrote several hundred poems. A. E. Thompson sums up Simpson's work load by referring to "his pulpit and platform work, his pastoral duties, his ministry for the sick, his lectures in the Institute [Nyack College], his convention tours, his correspondence, his editorial labors, his preparation of books, his production of hymns, and his executive responsibilities." And Thompson adds, "For him there was no such possibility as leisure."

These two lives expose the error of the notion that it is impossible to be both busy and spiritual. Wesley was known as "the busiest man in England"; yet he was a man of enormous spiritual power. Simpson's days were crammed with activities; yet he exuded a spiritual influence that was almost palpable.

I do not know enough about John Wesley to try to describe what drove him to work so hard. I think I understand, at least a bit, Simpson's heart and mind.

Simpson considered every day of his life to be a gift from God and felt that not one minute should be wasted on trivial things. He expressed this idea in one of his poems:

No time for trifling in this life of mine;
   Not this the path the blessed Master trod,
But strenuous toil; each hour and power employed,
   Always and all for God.

Simpson also was motivated by a consciousness that the time is too short and the needs around us are too great to permit any wasted time on meaningless activities or trivial pursuits. Another stanza says it:

Time swiftly flies; eternity is near
   And soon my dust will lie beneath the sod.
How dare I waste my life or cease to be
   Always and all for God.

I find it hard to argue with such an outlook. Perhaps a great many more of us would get much more done for Christ if we were gripped by the same convictions that motivated Wesley and Simpson.

A Balanced Attitude
toward Our Bodies

In our day concern for physical fitness has become a form of idolatry. Millions of people adore the image of a lean, trim, finely toned physique. Billions of dollars are offered to this god in membership fees at fitness centers, in money spent on exercise equipment and in the costs of cosmetic surgery.

Devotion to this idol is encouraged every day by dozens of television commercials and by billboard and magazine ads. "Worship" services are held at the local weight-lifting studio or health spa. The television evangelists for this "religion" are the aerobic instructors who lead watchers through a regime of exercises accompanied by music. Its "bible" is the latest, best-selling diet book.

A Christian will not become a devotee of this false "fitness cult." He knows that no matter how carefully we eat and how regularly we exercise, eventually our bodies begin to wear out and break down. The idol will begin to crumble, and anyone who has put faith and hope in physical fitness is bound eventually to be disappointed.

Also, the Christian is always aware that the soul is far more important than the body. Jesus warned us against an excessive concern with the physical. "Do not be afraid of those who kill the body but cannot kill the soul," He said. "Rather, be afraid of the one who can destroy both soul and body in hell" (Matthew 10:28). It is the condition of the inner man, not the outward, that will determine the shape of our characters and our eternal destinies.

Moreover, we will someday receive new bodies. First Corinthians 15:53 tells us, "The perishable must clothe itself with the imperishable, and the immortal with immortality." We need not be overly concerned with our present bodies because we will soon have new ones.

On the other hand, Christians should not ignore and neglect

our bodies. Some of the things taught by false religions are right, and to a degree the emphasis of the physical-fitness cult is proper.

God made the human body. That alone makes it worthy of respect.

Additionally, while it is true that the soul is more important than the body, the two are so intimately related that the condition of one affects the other. Therefore our spiritual condition tends to be affected adversely by poor physical health.

Also, God the Holy Spirit now dwells within those who have come to God through Christ. That means our bodies are His dwelling place. First Corinthians 6:19 says to Christians, "Do you not know that your body is a temple of the Holy Spirit, who is in you, whom you have received from God?"

That verse appears in a passage which tells the Christian to flee from sexual immorality. But obviously, if the Christian's body is a temple for the indwelling Holy Spirit all abuse and misuse of the body should be avoided.

We should be careful about what we eat or drink. Anything harmful should be left alone. Admittedly, virtually every kind of food and drink seems under suspicion these days. But we can be careful without being paranoid about this.

We should be careful about how much we eat. Obesity is unattractive. It leads to heart trouble and high blood pressure. Excess weight is like piled up snow on top of the temple of the Holy Spirit that should be removed before the roof caves in.

We should exercise. We bring breakdown and illness upon ourselves by not keeping fit. Then our usefulness to God is limited, and money we could give to His work is wasted on medical care and medicines.

We do not worship the body. We do not make physical fitness a religion. But we do care about what shape we are in. Paul prayed that our whole spirit, soul *and body* be blameless (1 Thessalonians 5:23). First Corinthians 6:20 says, "Honor God with your body."

We shall have new bodies someday. Until then we should take good care of the one we have.

Addicted to
Noise

The silence was deafening. I was home alone. Though I was not watching it, the television set was turned on. Suddenly, there was a power outage in the neighborhood. The television set went off. The blower on the furnace ceased operating. Because few cars pass our house, there was no street noise. Even the neighborhood dogs were silent. The house was deathly still.

After finding and lighting some candles, I sat for some time in that strange silence. And in those moments I became aware how addicted I have become to noise.

In the morning while brushing my teeth and shaving, I listen to National Public Radio news. I have another radio in my bedroom so that I can continue to listen to the news while I get dressed. When I go into the kitchen for breakfast, I turn on the radio.

As I drive to work the car is filled with either music or news from the radio. The day at my office is punctuated with the sounds of people's voices, telephone conversations and the noise of business machines. Also, I have a radio at my desk, and sometimes I play soft music while I work.

In the evening, at home, the television set blares out the play-by-play description of some sporting event or musicians presenting a concert. Or a deep-voiced narrator describes the migration patterns of elephants in Africa or the plight of some endangered species, and television anchor people once more crank out the news. The telephone jangles, and some telemarketing salesperson makes his pitch. If guests come for dinner, the stereo plays in the background.

I do not quite understand it, but on Sunday afternoons I can fall sound asleep while watching a sporting event on television. However, if my wife comes into the room, finds me sleeping and turns off the set, I immediately awaken.

I have become addicted to noise.

I do not think that I am, in this respect, all that unusual. Department stores and grocery markets fill their aisles with background music. Joggers listen to taped music as they exercise. The television set operates in the average American home for seven and a half hours a day. Kids walk down the street carrying tape players, and cars that pull up alongside me at red lights regularly have their radios blaring. I doubt that any generation in the history of the world has been so saturated with sound.

Little wonder that few of us ever hear the voice of God.

The Scriptures are full of admonitions to wait on the Lord, to be still in order to know Him. The ancient prophet heard God in the still, small voice.

However, few of us ever allow ourselves any moments of silence, and God's still voice is drowned out by the racket around us. Even when we go to church, the din that pervades the sanctuary before the service starts allows us little opportunity to become aware of God's presence and to listen for His voice.

Many of us are conscious of personal spiritual weaknesses. Some Christians are out of the will of God. What passes for Christianity at times seems utterly untouched by Divine influence. I wonder how much such tragic deficiencies in contemporary Christian experience are due to our failure to allow God any opportunity to speak to us. Our addiction to noise may be costing us a great deal more than we realize.

E. May Grimes's hymn says,

Speak, Lord, in the stillness,
While I wait on Thee;
Hushed my heart to listen,
In expectancy.

For the words Thou speakest,
They are life indeed;
Living bread from heaven,
Now my spirit feed!

What stillness? Where does one find any opportunity for the kind of experience this hymn describes? When was the last time you or I really waited upon the Lord in genuine quietness?

Prayer
Warriors

Recently, I was with a pastor and two missionaries. We were discussing the importance of prayer. And each of us spoke of knowing someone who is what I call a prayer warrior.

A prayer warrior is an individual, often but not necessarily a woman, who carries on an extensive ministry of prayer in support of the Lord's work around the world. She (or he) prays regularly for her family members, but her circle of concern is much larger.

She intercedes for people in the church of which she is a part—for the sick, for new Christians, for the youth and children. She prays for the church services and other activities. She upholds the church leaders and their families, especially the pastor or pastors.

Beyond that she remembers others involved in the Lord's work—other pastors, evangelists and teachers. And she prays for missionaries.

Each of the persons with whom the pastor, the two missionaries and I are acquainted knows specific missionaries, keeps track of their situations, remembers the names of their children, secures as much information about them as possible and prays fervently about the particular needs of the workers. And each does so consistently and systematically.

Such an individual's ministry may not be widely known. A prayer warrior may be unable, because of age or infirmity, to attend many public church services. He or she is not likely to receive any earthly recognition or reward.

Yet it is impossible to overstate the importance of the prayer warrior's ministry. Prayer puts a wall of protection around those for whom we intercede. Prayer supplies strength to those who labor for Christ. Prayer pushes back the forces of darkness and opens doors for the entrance of gospel light. Prayer invites the operations of God's Spirit upon situations of need and calls down divine power upon the preaching of the gospel.

Christian ministries involve warfare against demonic forces and satanic strategies. The devil seeks to keep doors closed upon yet unevangelized areas. He tries to turn people away from the truth. He seeks to bring affliction, discouragement and moral failure into the lives of Christian workers. He tries to stop the proclamation of the gospel. But the great and effective weapon of the Christian against all of Satan's efforts is prayer. So those who regularly employ prayer against the enemy make an enormous difference in the progress of the Lord's work.

Such prayer is not easy. There is nothing glamorous or self-enriching about seeking God for others in private intercession. Those who carry on such a ministry must fight against distractions and endure weariness. They make personal sacrifices of time and effort they might otherwise spend on themselves.

The choir director hears the results of his work. The teacher finds in the response of his pupil a reflection of what he has accomplished. The pastor can measure the effects of his ministry by the growth of his church. The janitor sees his clean church building; the church secretary sees her carefully typed letters; the missionary watches people come to Christ. But the prayer warrior very well may have to wait until she gets to heaven to learn what her prayers have accomplished.

Only God knows for sure how many have taken this ministry upon themselves. But I believe prayer warriors are few and far between. We have become addicted to creature comforts. We live in an age of convenience. Few are willing to spend the hours, bear the burdens and make the sacrifices that fervent intercession demands.

But without the backing of solid, faithful prayer, Christian workers go forth like an army without heavy artillery. They are like road builders without bulldozers. They are like fighters without water.

The supreme need of this hour is not for additional professional Christian workers, better strategies or more money. The Church needs more than anything else people who know how to lay hold of God in fervent prayer. If we have sufficient prayer, all our other needs will be met.

Hats Off to
Some Heroines

She is a widow, lives alone and still drives her own car. She is in church every Sunday morning (except when she is visiting her son or daughter who live in distant cities) and most Sunday nights. She does not teach Sunday school (though she has in the past). She is not a church officer. She was once a leader of the women's group, but now she just helps out wherever she is needed.

Helping out means working on the quilt the women's group is making for a missionary, cutting stamps from old envelopes so they can be sold to raise money for missionary radio and sending cards to those on the church's shut-in and sick list. She takes a turn in the church nursery, though the next morning she feels in her back the effects of lifting those kids. She also likes to help in the kitchen during church suppers, though the younger women often shoo her out, saying she did her part in earlier years and now she should be waited on by others.

She assists several people in her neighborhood. She often prepares a meal for a woman whose arthritis severely limits her ability to care for her own needs. Before she goes shopping she checks to see if the older woman two doors away needs any groceries. She has volunteered several times to watch the preschool child of a young mother.

She likes her church's services but not all the new music. She cannot quite get used to reading the words of the songs on a wall or clapping during choruses. She misses some of the "old" hymns. But she does not criticize. After all, she thinks, the younger people have a right to sing the kinds of songs they like. When others complain to her about all the new music, she says, "The church cannot plan everything it does just to please the old fogies like us."

She is a bit baffled by the exuberance of the young people in the church, by the way they dress and by their music. But she loves them, and they know it. After church services you often will see two or three of them talking to her. She always encourages them and thanks them for being a part of the congregation. She is a kind of grandmother to some of the church kids whose real grandmothers live miles away.

On occasion she has heard some criticisms of the pastor floating around the church. But she deliberately has avoided as much of such talk as possible. He is not the greatest preacher in the world, but she feels the church is fortunate to have a pastor who believes the Bible is God's Word and who is honest and upright. He was helpful to her when her husband died, and the funeral service was comforting. He does not visit her every week nor even every month. But this is OK because she agrees that he should be looking after people with greater needs.

She prays for the pastor every day, and she prays for other people in her church, particularly the new people who are attending its services. She prays for her neighbors, and she prays for missionaries. Several missionaries send her their prayer letters, and more should. She takes those letters seriously and brings every need they mention to the Lord until she senses that the prayer has been answered.

If people knew what she gave to the Lord's work, they would be amazed. Her husband's insurance paid off the mortgage and cared for the funeral expense, but little more. She is on a fixed income that allows for no luxuries. Yet she gives more to the church and to missions than a lot of the more affluent families in the church. And somehow she manages to find money to give to special needs that come along.

This is not a description of an actual person whom I know. She is a composite of several different individuals. But I have seen people like this in many churches. Congregations all across North America (and probably in other countries, too) are blessed with one or several unselfish, loving, saintly women. Their nonjudgmental, affirming, patient, generous spirit is like a precious perfume. They are a pastor's delight and a blessing to the whole church.

Thank God for such individuals. Their worth cannot be measured. May their tribe increase.

4

Discussing the Church

The Power
of the Church

A few days ago I had in my hands a brochure that described a certain community and listed its assets. It was designed to attract businesses to that area, and so it reported on those industries, organizations, educational institutions and cultural events that were likely to impact the community's future. No churches or religious groups were mentioned in the brochure.

I should not have been surprised at this omission. Increasingly the place of the church in the life of a community is being disparaged or ignored. Religious information is disappearing from local newspapers. Local governments feel little obligation to respect the interest of religious institutions in zoning practices and local statutes. In most places sporting events and business practices no longer avoid direct conflict with church activities. More and more churches are looked upon as innocuous relics of earlier, unenlightened eras that continue to flourish only because a fringe minority need their support for their immature psyches.

But the Church remains the most significant institution on the face of this earth.

Granted, those who make up the church are not, generally, the intellectually elite of the community. Admittedly, they are seldom the most affluent or politically powerful. Church members may not be the most sophisticated or the most well-known members of society. And people who evaluate an institution by these measures understandably will misjudge the significance of the Church.

However, the Church's power is derived from an entirely different source. The Church's might is due entirely to the indwelling presence of the living, triumphant Christ.

Fifty days after His Resurrection from the dead and 10 days after His ascension into heaven, Christ came back to earth in the Person of the Holy Spirit to indwell the lives of His disciples. Today, wherever a group of believers meets together for worship, fellowship and service, Christ is there.

Most people in Christ's day badly underestimated His influence. They saw only the external things—His ordinary background, His low social status, His poverty, His lack of an officially bestowed position. But the eternal Son of God dwelled in Jesus of Nazareth. Consequently, the religious life, the social conditions, even political structures were dynamically affected by the teaching and the other activities of this Man.

According to Ephesians 1:23, the Church is the Body on earth through which Christ comes into fullness, a full manifestation of His influence and power. Thus the Church, through the life of Christ it possesses within, is ever a tremendously significant force wherever it exists.

Because Christ alone is the source of the Church's strength, we must resist the temptation to try to gain the world's approbation by striving after greater intellectual respectability, political standing, social status or material wealth.

As believers become an increasingly despised group of people, we can be intimidated. We may tend to be embarrassed by the disdain with which we are regarded. We therefore may feel we must enhance our image financially or prove our prowess intellectually. In recent years we have been told that the Church must demonstrate its political clout. We are happy to have among us people of position in society because we feel this will raise our standing in the eyes of our world.

But our ability to influence this world does not depend upon such things. If we spend our energies trying to meet the world's measures of greatness, we will lose our ability to impact this world for God. The Church's power comes from the indwelling Christ. Therefore we must exalt Him, put all our resources at His disposal and let His life flow out from us to others.

Recently, a sports commentator said that a star football player's knee injury had done what opposing teams could not do; it had stopped him. The only thing that can stop the Church is our failure to give Christ a spiritually healthy, fully committed Body through which He can work in this world. Christ's life flowing through the company of the redeemed is a force against which the gates of hell cannot prevail.

Responding to Our
Changing Society

Rapid social change has created an enormous challenge for the Church of Jesus Christ in the last decade of the 20th century.

In the past, most evangelical congregations thought of themselves as close-knit families, and preaching strongly emphasized the responsibility of church members to relate intimately with one another in order to build up each other in the faith. A study by the Barna Research group found that today most single people and many young marrieds lack a felt commitment to any single congregation and operate from an essentially self-centered perspective. Consequently, they go to several different churches on an "as-needed" basis in order to satisfy a wide range of personal needs. Indeed, one church leader observes that the husband may like one church for its men's program and the wife another for opportunities offered to women, while the kids attend yet a third church for its exciting youth program.

Most evangelical church services center around a highly biblical, didactic sermon 30 to 45 minutes in length. Yet reputable psychologists have discovered that in our information-saturated age people have developed what one writer calls "overload amnesia." People increasingly hear more than they understand, forget quickly and resist learning more. Consequently, people confronted with in-depth teaching in large doses are likely to "hear" little of it and remember less.

As they face such significant sociological changes, churches can react in two inappropriate ways. They can rigidly maintain traditional approaches and emphases, refusing to "compromise" in any way with the spirit of the age. Viewing such things as set times for services, a traditional sermon length or a particular form of worship as having almost biblical authority, they can continue to do the same things the same way, year after year. However, such churches may fail to appeal to this generation

83

and attract few if any to their message and ministry.

On the other hand, churches may ignore biblical teaching concerning the church's nature and purpose, opt for "whatever works" and give people what they want whether or not it is what they need. In this case they may fill their facilities with people and activities but end up with congregations full of carnal Christians who bear little resemblance to New Testament believers.

Churches today must react to the changes in society in less radical ways. My suggestions for facing up to this challenge are as follows:

• First, church leaders must consider the nature and purpose of the church. They must decide what are its reasons for existence and determine how best it can achieve those objectives.

• Second, the truths concerning the church taught in the New Testament should be recognized as unassailable. The list of absolutes for every church includes observance of the ordinances, corporate worship, Bible teaching, evangelistic activities, service to community, involvement in world missions and mutual care among believers.

• Third, church leaders should study the needs of those to whom it seeks to minister. The church must scratch people where they itch.

• Fourth, church leaders must be willing to evaluate critically every activity to determine if it has biblical sanction and is serving a valuable end. A church can spend a great deal of time and energy engaged in activities that really have little part in making the church what it ought to be.

• Fifth, change ought to be introduced with caution. Change for change's sake has little value. All the possible implications should be considered. Some sense of consensus among the congregation should be sought.

That last ideal may be the most difficult to achieve. But seldom before has the church faced such rapidly changing conditions. To continue to serve God effectively a local congregation must have careful, thoughtful and creative direction.

The Dangers
of Worship

The "missing jewel" has been found. In 1961, speaking to a gathering of pastors of the Associated Gospel Churches of Canada, Dr. A. W. Tozer called worship the missing jewel of the evangelical church. But in recent years in churches across North America, Christian people have become increasingly aware of the importance of praise. This matter has been given primary attention by those who plan church services, and people are involving themselves more intensely in exercises of outpoured adoration to the Lord.

Granted, there are differences of opinion among Christians as to the forms in which corporate worship should be expressed. Changes that have been introduced in some places have provoked controversy. But clearly, congregation after congregation is giving primacy to worship.

No one is happier about this development than I. Those people who were in churches I pastored before I became an editor know I repeatedly preached on the importance of worship and passionately pleaded for people to participate in sincere expressions of thanksgiving, honor and exaltation to God. I therefore find it somewhat strange now to be warning about the dangers of an overemphasis on worship.

But I must do so. Satanic influences and the tendencies of carnal human nature often combine to spoil good things. And without discernment and care even an entirely appropriate emphasis on worship can be turned into something detrimental to our lives and to our churches.

We must be careful not to lose *the proper focus of worship.*

On occasion the United States government has sent humanitarian aid to impoverished foreign nations only to discover later that leaders in those nations have used that aid to better themselves and to provide luxuries for their own families. Similarly, God has given us opportunities, abilities and the assistance of the Holy Spirit to enable us to render worthy worship to Him. But our inherent selfishness makes us turn these things to our own advantage. We can worship in order to feel good. We can participate for the excitement the exercise affords us. We can begin, without realizing it, to seek primarily for emotional stimulation.

The focus of worship must be entirely upon the Lord. We worship to honor God, not to feel better. The measure of effective worship is how pleasing it is to God, not how much we enjoy it.

Sincere worship certainly involves our emotions. Tozer said, "A person who merely goes through the form and does not feel anything is not worshiping." But the purpose of worship is not to enhance our feelings; it is to exalt the Lord. If we do not carefully maintain that focus, we can delude ourselves into calling worship what is merely emotional self-indulgence.

Another word of caution: We must not limit *the scope of worship.* Several years ago an entertainer participated in a concert to raise money to help feed hungry people. The following week he was asked to help distribute food baskets to some needy families and refused. His critics rightly observed the gross inconsistency between his performance and his practice.

An overemphasis on corporate worship can lead to the same kind of inconsistency. It is possible for us to be so concerned about worship exercises that we convey the idea that sincere participation in heartfelt praise and earnest adoration ends our obligation to the Lord. But worship does not consist only of praise choruses and testimonies. And it does not stop at the church door. True worship involves not only singing "He is Lord" but also submitting to His Lordship in the way we use money, in the way we spend time and in the goals we pursue.

Taking seriously our obligation to give honor and praise to God in church services is good. But no matter how sincerely we feel and how fervently we express our praise in services and meetings, we have not worshiped God as we ought until we live out in deeds the love, honor and praise we ascribe to Him in words.

Form Is Not
the Crucial Issue

I recently had a conversation with someone who travels a great deal and, consequently, has an opportunity to observe quite a variety of churches. He shared with me his disappointment that so many services he attends are lifeless, dull, routine affairs. And if I interpreted his remarks correctly, he favors the inclusion of lively choruses, hand clapping, hand raising, testimonies and verbal expressions of "Amen" and "Praise the Lord"" in order to introduce some vibrancy and vitality into church services.

Just a few hours later I read a manuscript in which an author deplored the shallow, carnal quality of much of the lively worship he sees. And he advocated a formal worship style with stately hymns, structured liturgy and traditional elements to bring depth and sincerity into services.

This is not an argument for or against either of those opinions. Rather it is a comment on what I see as a fallacy in both points of view. Genuineness in worship does not depend upon form, and anyone who thinks that merely changing the style of a service will bring vitality to a meeting is mistaken.

Granted, someone used to pop music, demonstrative modes of expression and a casual lifestyle will be more responsive to and worship more easily in an exuberant, noisy, unstructured form. And similarly, someone who likes traditions, classical music and quiet will find it easier to enter into and be sincere about a liturgical service. But ultimately, the character of any worship depends upon the condition of the participants. If carnal, self-centered Christians engage in singing, clapping, dancing, shouting and raising their hands, the result will be a flamboyant exercise of the flesh. And to impose structure and form upon the worship of half-hearted, spiritually lethargic believers will produce a meaningless ritual.

Genuineness in worship does not depend upon a certain form, and I think we should stop arguing about styles and concern ourselves, instead, with the much more critical issue of the spiritual condition of our lives when we come together for services.

Three absolute essentials to proper, effective worship are reverence toward the Father, devotion to Christ and yieldedness to the Holy Spirit.

Dr. A. W. Tozer once defined worship as "A humbling but delightful sense of admiring awe and astonished wonder" (*Worship: The Missing Jewel of the Evangelical Church*, p. 9). Sometimes we think we have worshiped because we have been made to feel good, because we have gotten excited or because we have appreciated what we have heard. But we have not properly honored and exalted God unless, to use Tozer's words, "our spirits . . . stand silent and breathless . . . in the presence of that awful Wonder, that Mystery, that unspeakable Majesty, before whom the prophets used to fall, and before whom Peter and John and the rest of them fell down as if dead" (p. 10).

Vital worship also involves devotion to Christ. In John 4:23 Jesus said, "True worshipers will worship the Father in spirit and truth." Apart from Christ we are utterly condemned. All our eternal salvation depends entirely upon Him, and every blessing we experience flows to us through His grace. And when we are gripped by the truth of what Christ is to us, we will come before Him with hearts overflowing with praise and love.

Genuine worship also requires yieldedness to the Holy Spirit. Tozer said, "Only the Holy Spirit can enable a fallen man to worship God acceptably" (p. 18). More than a hundred times I have met with church leaders before a service to pray for the enabling and control of the Spirit in our lives as we prepared to lead a meeting. And every participant in worship must have that same enabling if he is to render worthy praise and honor to the Lord.

Whether you dress a corpse in blue jeans or a tuxedo, it is still dead. And whether they are in a contemporary, "charismatic" or traditional, liturgical-type service, spiritually dead people will not really worship. Let's put the emphasis where it ought to be, on substance rather than form.

We Have
Been Robbed

Christianity is a festive religion. It demands special celebration. Judaism, out of which Christianity sprang, was full of holidays and commemorations. The Hebrew people observed six major feasts during the year, some of which lasted days, and they engaged in other celebrations as well.

With that kind of background, it is not surprising that the Early Church adopted numerous annual commemorations. While the writings of the church fathers do not spell these out in detail, apparently early in its history, the Church began to celebrate Advent (the coming of Christ), Christmas, Epiphany (based on the visit of the wise men or, in some churches, a memorial of Jesus' baptism), Holy Week, Good Friday, Easter, Ascension Sunday and Pentecost (the coming of the Holy Spirit).

The Protestant Reformation in the 16th century did away with many of the saints days and "holy" days with which Roman Catholicism had encumbered the calendar during the Middle Ages. Some Protestant groups went so far as to ban almost all religious celebrations. The Puritans even frowned on the observance of Christmas in the American colonies.

Antipathy toward religious holidays has been reinforced among many 20th century evangelicals by an antiliturgical bias. A woman in a church I once pastored let me know she felt uncomfortable if I referred to Lent or to Holy Week. To her those terms suggested ritual observances that were substitutes for genuine, personal encounters with the Lord.

Consequently, many evangelical churches mark only Christmas, Easter, Good Friday and maybe Palm Sunday. And even the religious significance of Christmas and Easter has been eroded. Christmas has become for many evangelicals a family holiday as much as a church festival. And on Easter many will go only to a sunrise service so as to be able to rush off to visit relatives for an Easter family gathering and meal.

All this has robbed the Church of something of great value. Religious celebrations in the church can be greatly beneficial.

Holidays that commemorate events in the life of Jesus draw attention to Him, cause Him to be "lifted up" (John 3:14) and exalt Him in the midst of His people. Oddly enough, some of the people who object to the observance of Holy Week, Maundy Thursday or Ascension Sunday nevertheless expect the church to keep Mother's Day, Father's Day, Children's Day and other such man-centered celebrations.

Surely, churches also should celebrate with great joy the coming of the Holy Spirit at Pentecost. That was an advent of Deity to earth as surely as was the Christmas coming of Christ. Protestants ought to commemorate annually Reformation Day, to celebrate the recovery of the great doctrine of justification by faith.

Such observances invite God's people to express special praise and worship to God. Old Testament festivals often included times of fasting and special services in the temple. Christians, too, need specially designated times for meeting God and for worshiping Him.

Church holidays offer opportunities for visualizing the faith. We live in an increasingly visually oriented society. Celebrations invite us to use banners, drama, films, decorations—along with special music.

Special commemorations also offer outreach opportunities. We know that unchurched people will attend church for the special Christmas and Easter activities. Why not schedule a whole week of special meetings starting with Palm Sunday? Why not use Reformation Sunday as an opportunity for a film on Martin Luther, John Huss or John Wycliffe on Friday night, a dinner on Saturday night and a service built around the theme of justification by faith on Sunday?

Let us not be robbed of the rich opportunities afforded by religious celebrations to exalt Christ, enliven our services and reach out to others. Christianity is a festive faith. Let's make it so in our churches.

People Who
Prepare the Way

Recently, while he and I were discussing his church, a pastor referred to a layman in the congregation as "my John the Baptist." I am sure this pastor in no way meant to compare himself to Jesus Christ. Rather, he simply was reflecting the fact that every pastor needs those who prepare the way before him, those who by their work in the church enable him to minister more effectively.

That pastor's remark set me to thinking about people in the six churches I pastored before becoming an editor of a magazine. I remembered faithful elders and board members, obvious and elected leaders who were in major offices in those churches. However, I also recalled people who filled less conspicuous, less glamorous positions but whose work nevertheless prepared the way before me for the ministries I performed.

I thought of committed, diligent custodians. Many times I expressed gratitude to God as I walked into a well-cleaned, neatly arranged building on Sunday morning to find the doors already unlocked, the lights on, the heat regulated and everything prepared for the service. A custodian had been there, perhaps late the night before and certainly early that morning. And because he took care of those things, I could concentrate on the spiritual ministries I felt God gave to me for that day.

I thought of the people who ran the sound systems. Anyone who speaks in an auditorium that requires a P.A. system knows all too well how problems with the sound can utterly ruin a meeting. I still shudder at some of the bad experiences I have gone through. But I also recalled with warm gratitude people who dedicated themselves to keeping equipment in good working order, who prepared the system in advance and who monitored it during the service.

I thought of musicians—organists, pianists, choir directors, choir members and people who contributed to services with special music. The character of the music has a large impact on any meeting. I remembered with special appreciation musicians who made an effort to find out and to understand what I was trying to accomplish in the meeting and to arrange their participation to complement mine.

I thought of ushers. I can recall men who were in place well ahead of time and were always gracious, warm, friendly and alert. They tactfully kept late arrivals from distracting other worshipers, regulated the ventilation, handled disturbances and patrolled the precincts. Still, they were a part of the service, setting an example for others by their sincere participation.

Of course, I also remembered those who cared for the children who came to church. Praise the Lord for nursery attendants and for those who conduct children's church.

I have preached overseas to audiences filled with crying babies and restless children, and I have been amazed at how people in those other lands can block out these sounds and distractions while they listen. But North Americans cannot do this, so those who care for children while the pastor ministers to adults are a great blessing to him. And, of course, the children get far more out of an hour's activities that are designed according to their level of interest and understanding.

I am sure every pastor is most grateful for those who prepare the way before him by prayer. Nothing so makes or breaks a pastor's ministry than those who pray for him and for the church—or who fail to do so.

Recently, someone paid a public tribute to me, saying my preaching had inspired a number of young people to commit their lives to missionary service. But there is another angle to that story. In that church from which many of those young people came, a group of women prayed regularly that God would use the ministries of that church in a powerful way among its youth. Nothing I ever did or said would have impacted anyone had not the way been prepared by prayer.

John the Baptist and Jesus were a team. And good lay support and faithful pastoral work constitute teamwork that the Lord can use today. I hope many pastors are as blessed with good helpers as I was.

Whatever Happened to Testimonies?

I do not often hear people sharing personal testimonies in church services any more. This may be a vital part of the life of some congregations, but churches with which I have been associated or that I have attended in recent years give little opportunity to people to publicly praise the Lord for personal spiritual victories.

There are perfectly understandable reasons for this diminished emphasis on testimonies. In most places the Sunday morning worship service must not last more than one hour. And with necessary hymns, Scripture readings, announcements, prayers and the sermon already crowded into that time frame, there is no room for anything else.

Individuals could tell of what God has done for them at a Sunday evening or midweek service. But less than half of most congregations ever attend any other than the Sunday morning meeting. Consequently, on Sunday nights or at the midweek prayer meeting, the same faithful few rehearse their blessings, and those who would benefit most from sharing a testimony or from hearing others testify are not there.

In some churches opportunities for personal praise have been abused. I once heard a young man publicly describe in embarrassing detail the difficulties his wife had experienced in childbirth. I have listened to people indulge in exercises of self-pity. Some individuals take far too long to say what they want to say. Some testimonies are made up of virtually meaningless cliches, and I do not think the repetition of half-sincere religious jargon has much value.

Yet the church today is poorer for the absence of individual reports of what God is doing for His people. Public testimonies *confirm* the work of God within us. It is very important for a person who has trusted in Christ as personal Savior to openly acknowledge his or her decision. Romans 10:9 says, "If you confess with your mouth, 'Jesus is Lord,' and believe in your heart that God raised Him from the dead, you will be saved."

It is equally necessary to confirm spiritual victories in one's Christian walk by public praise. Overcomers in heaven are said to have prevailed against Satan "by the blood of the Lamb / and by the word of their testimony" (Revelation 12:11).

Also, we *teach* each other by our declarations of what God has done in our lives. A woman once told me, "I began to tithe after I heard a fellow believer describe his experience (about tithing)." In periods of revival God often uses public acknowledgments of victory to persuade others to wholly follow the Lord.

In addition, testimonies *encourage* fellow believers. Someone once complained to me that healings did not occur in his church. He said, "I never hear of anyone in our congregation receiving the kind of divine deliverance that people in some other churches experience."

The significant word in his comment was "hear." I happened to know that a woman in his church was healed marvelously of a growth on her neck and shoulder. But because this was not publicly acknowledged, few in the church ever knew of her deliverance. And others who might have been influenced by such a testimony to trust God for their physical problems did not receive that encouragement.

I am not sure how orderly, dignified, edifying personal praise can be worked in our church services in a way beneficial to all. If I were a pastor I would try offering such an opportunity at the close of the morning service—after the sermon and before the benediction.

People can be instructed to keep their expressions short and Christ-centered and in good taste. They can be directed to report specific instances of spiritual advance or divine deliverance. Somehow, someway, vital periods of personal praise belong in the life of the church.

Psalm 145:4 says, "One generation will commend your works to another; / they will tell of your mighty acts." Let us do this among our fellow believers.

Why Don't We Kneel Anymore?

I am disappointed that in the religious circles in which I move almost no one kneels to pray anymore.

I am talking about prayer times during church services, small group prayer meetings and the moments spent in prayer at church committee sessions. Occasionally, people stand for prayer. Most often they sit.

I recently attended an hour-long prayer meeting in which about 30 people interceded for the Lord's work around the world. During part of that time we all prayed together. The rest of the time we were in small groups of three or four people each. During the whole hour we sat while we prayed. We did not kneel.

I am aware that the Bible does not require that prayer be offered to God from any particular posture. I know that God hears a sincere prayer from a sitting person as readily as from someone who kneels. I am aware that our heart attitude when we pray is far more important than our posture.

Yet our body language often reflects our inner attitudes. And I wonder if sitting rather than kneeling to pray does not say something about our whole approach to this important spiritual exercise.

Kneeling always has been an expression of reverence. Subjects kneel before their monarchs. Solomon knelt when he prayed, "O LORD, God of Israel, there is no God like you in heaven or on earth" (2 Chronicles 6:14). Psalm 95:6 associates kneeling with reverence:

Come, let us bow down in worship,
let us kneel before the LORD our Maker.

And certainly the Lord ought to be approached with fear and honor.

But awe toward the Lord is conspicuously missing from much

95

of contemporary religious activity. Most Christians come into worship services no differently than they would enter a restaurant. We treat things set apart to Him—His day, His house and His Word—with little concern about their sacredness.

I wonder if our disinclination to kneel when we pray is not a symptom of this lack of genuine reverence for God. Would not a proper appreciation of His majesty and glory drive us to our knees?

This posture also is an expression of supplication. The captain sent by the king of Samaria fell on his knees before Elijah to beg for the lives of his men (2 Kings 1:13). People who sought help from Jesus did so on their knees (see Matthew 17:14; Mark 1:40, 10:17).

Members of this egotistical and self-centered generation act sometimes as if we deserve God's blessings and have every right to heaven's help. But in fact we in ourselves are worthy of nothing. We have no ground in ourselves upon which to expect anything from the Lord. And should not this recognition force us into the posture of supplication?

I remember seeing a student from a foreign country in an American college dormitory standing as he studied his history textbook. He explained to me that he was more mentally alert when he stood. His intense desire to learn compelled him to study in a less comfortable posture.

My observations are that people who feel burdened and are gripped by a spirit of travail in intercession will kneel before the Lord. When Jesus prayed in great agony in Gethsemane, He was kneeling (Luke 22:41). A comfortable sitting posture does not seem consistent with great concern, deep feelings and passionate pleadings before the Lord. And if there was ever a day when we ought to be burdened and intensely concerned, it is now!

Someone may accuse me of majoring on something minor, of making a mountain out of a molehill, of creating an issue of a triviality. I would agree were it not that I see our posture in prayer as a reflection of a much deeper problem—our lack of reverence, humility and intensity. When we are dead serious about prayer, we will have trouble doing it sitting down.

Who Said So?

Many years ago I heard a British aristocrat, who was on a television talk show, say that a gentleman ought to never wear brown shoes after 4:00 P.M. But tell that to a young man today and he is sure to say, "Why not?"

I was taught that when seated with others for a meal, one should not begin eating until everyone at the table has been served. But offer that as a rule to younger people today and their reply is likely to be, "Who said so?"

People today, generally speaking, care little for traditions and do not respect authority. And obviously, some of this casting off of the restraints of the past is justified. If, for example, a man wants to wear sneakers with a tuxedo, what harm is there in his doing so?

However, this trend of radical individualism can be carried too far. And it is especially harmful within the church. There is a place for the traditional in religion, and authority must undergird Christianity. I want to discuss tradition in this essay and speak of authority in the next.

There is no question that radical individualism has invaded the church. Statements such as "we have always done it this way in the past" carry almost no weight at all. "Do your own thing" has become a lifestyle formula even for people within the family of believers.

We cannot, however, discard all religious traditions and conventions without doing harm to ourselves and to Christ's Kingdom.

Across the centuries godly people have learned by experience that certain practices and standards enable the church to be what it ought to be and to do what it ought to do. I am thinking of such traditional things as respect for the clergy, reverence in church services, membership in and loyalty to a local church and putting our tithes into the local congregation. I am talking about customs that promote order and respect for the opinions of others.

It is easy to discard practices that we do not find especially appealing while forgetting that those activities may be a source of great help and blessing to someone else. It is very easy for young people to look at taboos that governed the lives of Christians in an earlier generation as irrelevant and even, in some cases, ridiculous. Yet some of these convictions about conduct were hammered out on the anvil of bitter experiences.

Radical individualism represents an inordinate pride in one's own wisdom. Surely we are on safer ground to respect the traditions we have inherited from the past than to always assume that we can decide for ourselves how we ought to act.

How, then, can those of us who respect tradition combat the excesses of radical individualism? Not by confrontation and controversy. Not by caustic condemnation. Rather, we must conduct ourselves with such integrity and godliness that we earn the right to be heard.

A few years ago I delivered some lectures at a seminary. I have a strong educational background with an earned doctorate. I have had more than 30 years of pastoral experience. I have achieved some stature in my denomination. I soon discovered, however, that all that meant very little to those young people. They did not hesitate to challenge what I was teaching. I found that I had to make them appreciate me before they would listen to my opinions.

No matter how proven our propositions, no matter how logical the point of view that we espouse, the bottom line for people around us is their respect for us as individuals. A person who is loved will be given a hearing, no matter how old-fashioned he may be.

The Church of Jesus Christ must not be hindered by the excesses of radical individualism. Those who want to "do their own thing" and demand change need humility. Those who want to see certain conventions and traditions maintained must act in integrity and love. Then we will change what needs to be changed and leave in place those things that deserve to remain.

Do Your Own Thing

In present-day society, "do your own thing" has become more than an advertising slogan or a casual cliche. It has become a philosophy of life for a great many people. Rules of etiquette, traditional forms of behavior and established customs mean very little to the modern generation.

But nonconformity can be harmful when it is carried too far, particularly in religion. In the previous essay, I talked about our tendency these days to reject convention and cast aside traditions. But more seriously, today individualism is undermining the authority of the Word of God, even among those who claim to be evangelical Christians.

Incredibly, some believers seem to feel that lying is OK in certain circumstances and that dishonesty in some cases can be excused. An active member of an evangelical church attended a high school reunion. Later that day she called her husband to say that she would not be coming home. She had met an old high school flame and decided to leave her husband and go live with this man. She claimed she was doing the right thing because she did not love her husband any more. George Barna, in his book *Absolute Confusion*, reports that only 69 percent of evangelical Christians claim the Scriptures as their primary authority for making ethical and moral decisions.

Because the idea of hell seems distasteful to them, some Christians have begun to suggest it may not exist. Because it seems intolerant, some Christians find it hard to say that Christ is the only way to God. I have heard Christians raise the possibility of reincarnation, something clearly inconsistent with the teaching of Scripture. Obviously, a great many people who claim to be Christians think that they have a right to decide for themselves what to believe.

However, we must have no illusions about the absolute authority of the Word of God. Genuine Christian experience is established upon the teaching of the Scriptures. Each of us must be convinced of the verity of God's Word. And we must understand that all beliefs and practices must be governed by the Word of God.

I am aware that people today have difficulty accepting anything as absolute. Young people especially do not want to be told that they must believe certain things or act in certain ways. However, we have no options when it comes to that which is clearly taught in God's Word. We do not bring our feelings, our judgments nor our conclusions to the Scriptures. We bow before the Word and submit to its precepts.

But how can we reestablish the authority of the Word of God among believers? How can we replant this rock where floods of radical individualism have moved it aside? We must do so by preaching the Word, teaching it and by causing it to be read. Francis Schaeffer, in *Escape from Reason*, said, "It is possible to take the system the Bible teaches, put it down in the marketplace of the ideas of men and let it stand there and speak for itself."

Unfortunately, a lot of preachers are presenting pop psychology and human testimonies. Donald W. McCullough, in an article in *Leadership* magazine, tells of a layman who came to him after a recent Sunday morning and said in a very loud voice, "I hated your sermon!" But then, a few seconds later in a softer voice the same man said, "But don't stop preaching the Word, because I need it." Like it or not, willing to accept it or not, people need the Word of God, and the Bible will establish its own authority in that community where it is clearly proclaimed.

Additionally, people must be encouraged to read the Scriptures. There is a direct correlation between our position with respect to the authority of the Bible and the time we spend reading it. The Bible will establish its own authority in the heart of that individual who explores its pages.

A person today may, with some justice, challenge his teachers in school, question the validity of rules of etiquette and even wonder at the rightness of some man-made laws. But he must not deny the absolute authority of God's Word.

Our Heated
Controversies

We should not be surprised that heated controversies occur among Christians. Sparks and flare-ups are almost inevitable because the issues we discuss are of great consequence.

Take the matter of worship styles (about which some strong differences of opinion are being expressed by people associated with evangelical churches).

If we were considering the proper apparel to wear to a symphony concert, only fools would care very deeply about the final decision. A determination concerning which dressing to serve on the salad to be put before guests coming to dinner would merit no serious argument.

But worship to the Christian is a matter of great moment. We understand that we are approaching the great Creator of the universe. We see Him as worthy of our best possible expression of adoration. We want to offer up our praise and thanksgiving in the most appropriate and effective way.

We bring, therefore, an understandable intensity to a discussion of worship styles. We rightly feel strongly about this matter. And our opinions are likely to be delivered with passion, perhaps even vehemence.

We must never lose our strong concern about such important matters. A worship service is infinitely more than a symphony concert or a dinner party. An apathetic attitude concerning our services is a far greater evil than being overzealous in pushing our personal points of view.

But our passions in religious discussions must be tempered by good sense. We tend to be carried by our strong feelings to extremes.

In the past, people who have insisted on the importance of beauty in worship sometimes have ended up with services in which aesthetic satisfaction has become more important than communication with Deity. Some have carried so-called "free-

101

dom of expression" in worship to the extreme of personally satisfying emotional "orgies" that may not address God at all.

We need to consider formal or informal styles, structured or spontaneous expressions, hymns or choruses, much preaching or little, raising hands or kneeling with bowed heads and the like with humility. Who are any of us to decide what God appreciates? And even if we say that we have based our understanding of worship on what we are taught in Scripture, let us acknowledge the imperfectness of our understanding of the Book.

We must not exalt personal preferences to the level of principle. We perpetually tend to make our experiences normative. We feel that because we respond to a certain style this must be the correct one.

But different people may worship God effectively in very different ways. Variety in individual temperaments and tastes is as much a part of God's creation as the colors that create the splendor of fall foliage. As a result of their God-given personalities, then, some people will express themselves toward the Lord with outspoken praise or tears or smiling faces while others will be utterly still and deeply solemn.

Cultural background, education and degree of spiritual maturity also affect the manner in which a sincere person seeks to approach God. And some accommodation must be made in our attitudes for these differences.

Let us also remember that what works is more important than what we enjoy. A man complained about the services of a certain church by saying that when he went there he was bored. I wanted to say in response (but I did not), "So what? The services are not arranged for your entertainment."

A lot of our opinions about proper worship reflect a greater concern about our personal satisfaction than about God's. The form and content of a service must focus on whether or not people are really brought into contact with the living God and whether or not praise, adoration and thanksgiving ascend from us to Him.

Let us continue to care deeply about religious issues. But let us conduct our discussions in an atmosphere of humility, tolerance and selflessness.

What to Do about
Pastor-Church Conflicts

According to a recently released study, conflicts between Southern Baptist congregations and their pastors are occurring with epidemic frequency. In one 18-month period 2,100 Southern Baptist pastors left their churches under fire.

This is not the only group having such problems. Leaders of virtually every denomination in North America report a surge of strife within their churches.

Several people with whom I have discussed this phenomenon have identified some of the causes of these conflicts. But I have heard few suggestions as to how this epidemic can be stopped. I want to venture into this area with some suggestions.

The simplest solution to all such problems is revival. If both clergy and laity were to humble themselves before God in repentance and seek deliverance from pride, selfishness and wrongheadedness, many disputes would cease.

But practical steps are needed also. These can resolve conflicts or, better still, head off such confrontations before they develop.

First, the entire church should come to a clear understanding (perhaps a written understanding) of the respective roles of every leader in the church. An effective pastor told me his church maintains a written manual (available to anyone in the congregation) that describes the responsibilities of each member of the pastoral staff, all officers and every committee.

Who decides the worship style? What if a majority on the governing board wants to open a child-care center and the pastor is dead set against it? To whom is the youth pastor accountable? Who chooses the choir director? Because widely varying opinions may exist within the congregation, such issues ought to be answered by a clearly drawn set of guidelines.

Denominational leaders may supply churches with biblical instruction concerning church government. But because churches vary so greatly in character, a denominational headquarters cannot impose rigid and detailed procedures. The local church must confront this matter.

Here is one possible approach: The pastor should draw up an outline of his duties and those of church officers. Lay leaders should do the same. Then a mutually acceptable set of guidelines can be adopted from these.

Limits of responsibility may change. I have noticed that sometimes a pastor who has served a congregation for 10 or more years begins to act as if the church were his personal property and makes more and more unilateral decisions concerning church life. At the same time the church may have an increasing number of strong, capable laymen who feel called of God to have a decisive part in what goes on within the congregation. At such a juncture, earlier guidelines may need to be revised.

When understandings about leadership roles have been reached and endorsed by the congregation, everyone should respect the structures of authority. The Bible clearly teaches that we are to be subject to those who are over us in the Lord (1 Thessalonians 5:12–13; Hebrews 13:17).

Today some people seem to have no hesitation in attacking church leaders and stirring up rebellion against constituted authority. Strong-minded individuals sometimes insist on pushing some personal agenda. Such activity is encouraged by the spirit of our age with its glorification of the individual, its self-centeredness and its disdain for government.

But this spirit is not of the Lord. Congregational life is to be characterized by respect, humility, patience and cooperation.

We may have strong opinions about how things should be done. We have a right to express those opinions in a constructive way to church leaders. But we also have a responsibility to shut our mouths and support the decisions of those in authority, even when things have not gone exactly according to our preferences.

The Lord of the Church is not pleased by strife within His Body. Let us take those steps necessary to avoid conflicts and to resolve them where they exist.

Helping Young People Remain Pure

A few years ago, a prominent superstar in the National Basketball Association suddenly announced he was retiring from basketball because a blood test showed him to be infected with the HIV virus, which causes AIDS. He also stated he would do what he could to encourage young people to practice safe sex. Presumably, he meant he would urge those involved in sexual relations with multiple partners to use condoms.

Many of us who listened to this player's press conference or saw news reports concerning what he said were sorry that he did not talk about the one, sure way for an individual to avoid infection through sex—abstinence from immoral sexual practices. Anyone who seriously wants to help young people avoid AIDS ought to say, "Do not engage in sexual activity outside of marriage." A simple application of biblical standards is the best and only genuine answer to this problem.

However, it is one thing to preach abstinence from illicit sex to young people and quite another thing to provide an atmosphere and activities in our churches that will encourage young people to remain sexually pure. Simply telling our kids to abstain is not enough.

Young people these days are bombarded with sex. Movies, television programs, books and conversations are filled with depictions of promiscuity. Most often such activity is portrayed as exciting and enriching; its bad consequences are almost never addressed.

Peer pressure on young people is enormous. Statistics about the sexual activities of junior and senior high youth indicate that sex is almost as common as listening to rock music or hanging out at a mall. When a young person tells his parent, "Everybody is doing it," he is not far from wrong.

These powerful influences cannot be offset alone by stern preaching from pastors or biblical warnings from Sunday school

105

teachers and youth leaders. Young people must be offered understanding, counsel and personal support from strong, older Christians. They must have an opportunity to associate with a peer group that reinforces their commitment to Christian standards. They must have plenty of opportunities to engage in wholesome activities as alternatives to the "fooling around" into which they might otherwise be drawn.

Unfortunately, many churches do not provide this kind of support to youth. A missionary on furlough and traveling from church to church said that most congregations he visited had few or no youth programs. He observed that some churches have a positive ministry to youth, but many do not.

Working with youth is difficult, and this is, perhaps, the problem. We find it far easier to preach to young people than to provide for them a dynamic program in our churches. We can criticize their music, dress, talk and tastes more readily than we can care about them and involve ourselves in their lives.

I am well aware that facilities for youth programs in churches are costly. I know that good youth workers are hard to find. I know that young people sometimes disappoint those who try to help them and try the patience of the most gracious pastor, Sunday school teacher or youth sponsor.

But a great danger is stalking today's youth. Precious kids are being drawn into destruction, and preaching abstinence is not enough to save them. I urge church leaders to take a long, hard look at the issue—what should we be doing for today's young people?

A Christmas Gift
for the Pastor

The matter of a Christmas gift or gifts from a church to its pastor or pastors is handled in a variety of ways. I know this from personal experience and from my conversations with other ministers.

Most commonly the church receives a special offering of money that is then presented to the pastor during the annual Sunday school Christmas program or at some other appropriate meeting during the Christmas season. Some churches use the money to buy a gift for the pastor and/or his family—a set of books, a computer, a microwave oven or some such thing.

Some churches do nothing officially and collectively, but individuals give their gifts, usually money, directly to the pastor. In other places the pastor receives nothing, either from the whole church or from individual members. I know of instances in which pastors who had become accustomed to receiving rather substantial Christmas remembrances found themselves in new places of service. Christmas passed and they got nothing.

Obviously, this is not a subject the pastor can raise at a board meeting. I, therefore, want to offer some suggestions. Even if everyone does not agree with what I propose, perhaps my comments will provoke a discussion of this issue among church leaders.

The pastor or pastors should be given a Christmas gift by the congregation. Business leaders, company executives, even assembly line employees commonly receive holiday bonuses. The pastor should be accorded this same expression of appreciation.

Generally pastors are far from being overpaid and can use extra money at holiday times.

The collection and presentation of such a gift encourages respect in the congregation for the office the pastor occupies. And in our day there is a declining sense of the sanctity of the pastoral office that should be restored. For these reasons and others the pastor should be given a Christmas gift.

It should, usually, be money. When I was a pastor, what I received usually helped to pay for gifts I purchased for others, so I was grateful for cash.

The gift should come from the church through its treasurer rather than from separate individuals. When gifts are given by individuals directly to the minister, he may be tempted to allow that gift to affect his attitude toward that person (and toward those who do not give him anything). People may feel that they have a right to deferential treatment because they know he knows they gave a substantial gift. It is better that all Christmas remembrances be given under the anonymity of a collective gift presented by the entire church. Individuals can still express their personal greetings to the minister and his family by a card.

Where a church has more than one pastor the money should be divided equally. The senior pastor may seem more worthy because of the larger responsibility he carries. However, other staff members are likely to receive smaller annual salaries. Therefore they may need the special gift more. I am sure no senior pastor will resent the fact that other staff members were given as much as he was.

I am not sure why so many church leaders feel that the collecting of this money should be kept secret from the pastoral staff. If a man has served a church more than one year, the annual holiday remembrance will not be a surprise. Yet church secretaries and treasurers will go to great lengths to hide from the pastor any indication that such an offering is being received. The secrecy, in my opinion, is unnecessary.

The Christmas gift should be presented publicly to the pastor or pastors (and his wife or their wives) at a church service. A public presentation says to all who see it that a church honors the pastoral office.

If your church does not remember its pastor or pastors at the Christmas season, I think your church leaders should read this essay. Even if my suggestions are not followed, this matter should be discussed by them.

5

Concerns about Society

Winning the Culture War

In a 1992 book called *Hollywood vs. America*, Michael Medved, a Jewish film and television critic, accuses moviemakers and television producers of attacking religion, glorifying brutality, undermining the family and deriding patriotism. Moreover, Medved contends, leaders in the entertainment industry seem determined to follow their own dark obsession with sex, violence and profanity despite the fact that these things are turning people off from movies.

Medved's book provides one more convincing piece of evidence in support of Harold 0. J. Brown's thesis in *The Religion and Society Report* that the United States is in the midst of a culture war. (And what he says also applies to Canada.) Brown refers to "a conjunction of forces and influences that all impel our culture towards one ultimate end, its own dissolution." Its goal is "to destroy spiritual, intellectual, and moral stability in the U.S." Its main target, he contends, is the Judeo-Christian tradition.

Without doubt, diabolical forces are at work in our society to undermine moral standards and negate the influences of religion. The question that remains is what should Christians do to counter these forces.

We care because we love our nation, and we know that current trends threaten our continued existence. As Harold Brown says, "A good measure of the civility that still exists in American society is dependent on the vestiges of Christianity and . . . it will not survive their disappearance." We care as well about what is happening because of the impact that the collapse of the U.S. and Canada would have upon the evangelization of the world. North America is still, by far, the major source of missionary activity on this globe.

For several years Christians have sought to counter the destructive forces of evil in organized political action groups like The Moral Majority and The Coalition for Family Values. We have

111

participated in marches, boycotts, letter-writing campaigns and rallies. We have tried to penetrate the media, political parties and the courts to bring Christian influences to these arenas.

Such efforts have done good. We might well be much worse off than we are now without them. But they have not been successful enough. The downward spiral has not stopped.

It is time to recognize and employ the ultimate solution. Both the Bible and history tell us how to combat the forces of moral decay and spiritual darkness. Second Corinthians 10:4 says, "The weapons we fight with are not the weapons of the world. On the contrary, they have divine power to demolish strongholds."

And how do we bring divine power to bear upon society? Social conditions in the early 18th century in England and America were remarkably similar to what they are today. However, preaching about these evils brought little change. Reform movements met with contempt. "So," says Gerald R. McDermott, in an article in the March 3, 1993, issue of *Alliance Life*, "in the 1720s and 1730s, after decades of feeling that true religion was dying, American and British evangelicals turned to prayer." Everywhere Christian people began to cry out to God concerning conditions around them.

At the same time, Christian societies, especially in England, sprang up to promote holiness in heart and life. People sought God with fervency of spirit. A kind of desperation for revival began to grip people everywhere.

As a result, God began to move through the Church in England and America with power. Christians were renewed. Thousands were converted. Whole communities were shaken to their foundations. "By the time it subsided," McDermott says, "the political and social cultures of the Anglo-American world had been forever changed."

Victory for right and truth in the current culture war must come through the power of God operating in His Church. And we must give God the opportunity to move again as He did before. It is time to get serious about prayer, about holiness and about revival.

Mislabeling Evil

A poll conducted by the Wirthlin Group revealed that many Americans misunderstand the term "pro-choice." Nearly half of those who indicated that they believe abortion should not be allowed except in cases of rape, incest or danger to the mother's life also identified themselves as being pro-choice. But this is the term that is used by those who advocate unrestricted abortions on demand.

We should not be surprised that people are confused. The term pro-choice is an entirely *inaccurate* expression for the position of those who use it to describe their views.

"Choice" is a nonspecific word with no inherent moral content. Choice can refer to something as harmless as deciding what pair of shoes to wear or whether or not to go out for dinner.

But the decision to have an abortion is a life or death matter that has long-term consequences to the psyche of the mother and fatal implications for the child who is being formed within her womb. It is much more than simply a choice. Those who believe that any mother should be allowed to destroy the life of her as yet unborn infant should call their view "pro-infanticide" or at least "pro-abortion."

"Pro-choice" also is an entirely inappropriate term. That expression suggests that sometime after a baby has been conceived and is growing within her a woman can decide then whether or not she wants to be a mother.

But a woman who has become pregnant has already made a choice. She agreed to sexual intercourse. (Obviously not in case of rape, but few of the several million abortions performed annually in North America involve the victims of rape.) The so-called pro-choice position, then, does not uphold a woman's right to choose but rather her right to avoid the consequences of choices she makes.

Moreover, the right to choose is not at all extended to the

other human being involved in an abortion—the child. Pro-choice really is anti-choice. It denies to another human being the opportunity to choose to live.

There is as well a degree of *hypocrisy* in the pro-choice des-ignation. If, as its advocates assert, there is no wrong in aborting a fetus, why do not they call their view pro-abortion? Why delib-erately use a milder sounding term? Is this not another instance of darkness dressing itself as light?

Euphemisms for evil are common. Homosexuals call them-selves gay. Adultery is referred to as having an affair or an indis-cretion. Terrorists call themselves freedom fighters. The fact that some other term is used to describe it is a kind of admission that the act is wrong.

Shakespeare said, "A rose by any other name would smell as sweet." And sin by any other name smells as foul. Keats said concerning death that he had "call'd him soft names in many a mused rhyme." But no soft names can disguise the tragedy of death.

Advocates of abortion should be honest enough to use terms that fairly describe their position. Christian journalists, preachers and teachers ought not to employ their fallacious slogans and designations. David O'Steen, executive director of the National Right to Life Committee, says, "Abortion advocates have used slogans like 'choice' to mislead millions of Americans and con-fuse the abortion debate."

We must cry out against such semantic abuse. And we must be careful always to speak clearly and specifically. The issue is *not* one of women's rights and choice. The issue is life or death for millions of children.

Wanted: Another Wilberforce

Two hundred years ago Great Britain was the world's leading slave-trading nation. In his book *God's Politician*, Garth Lean says, "The total number of slaves carried by the British in the eighteenth century is hard to estimate, but an American authority calculates they had supplied three million to the French, Spanish and British colonies by 1776" (pp. 2–3).

A few voices were raised in protest. John Wesley called slave trading "the execrable sum of all villainy." But because it was protected by law, this tragic traffic could be stopped only by parliamentary action. And slave trading was so widely regarded as indispensable to England's economic well-being that any politician who dared to push for abolition risked committing political suicide.

However, such a politician did appear on the scene. He was small in stature—5 feet, 4 inches tall and only 23 inches around the chest. In an attack upon his policies, James Boswell, the poet and biographer, referred to him as "Thou dwarf with big resounding name."

But measured by his courage, William Wilberforce was a giant. On October 28, 1787, he wrote in his journal, "God Almighty has set before me two great objects: The suppression of the slave trade and the reformation of manners." And for 20 years Wilberforce fought to change British law and do away with slavery.

He suffered repeated setbacks. He was vilified by his opponents. His life was threatened. His efforts were physically exhausting.

Still he persisted. And finally, on January 3, 1807, with his head in his hands and with tears streaming down his face, Wilberforce heard Parliament vote 283 to 16 for abolition.

Today, an even greater evil than slavery is being perpetuated daily throughout North America. It is abortion. And many signif-

115

icant voices are being raised in protest against the wholesale slaughter of millions of innocent, helpless, unborn babies.

Still, at the present time abortions are legal in the United States and Canada, and this evil will continue unchecked until the U.S. Congress and the Canadian Parliament take action against it.

These facts make me long to see some North American politician be courageous enough to devote his life to a crusade against abortion. Wilberforce delivered speech after speech against slavery in the British Parliament. He and his coworkers presented volumes of information in support of abolition. A print of a slave ship showing slaves packed as sardines in the hold was circulated with Wilberforce's blessing.

I wish some North American political leader would speak boldly in a legislative session, present the facts and bring this evil out into full view. He would be crucified by the media. His presentations would be distorted by reporters. He would be ridiculed by fellow legislators and vilified by segments of present day society.

But I believe a majority of North Americans would appreciate someone willing to take a strong stand for a just cause. Polls seem to indicate an ambivalence on the part of people in general about abortion. Most are against unlimited abortions. Still, most seem to favor a woman's right to choose whether or not she should continue to carry her child until it is born. I believe a strong leader could conduct our nations out of this confusion.

I am praying for the emergence of a modern-day Wilberforce. Garth Lean says of him, "Wilberforce lived that higher statesmanship that consists in serving not his own interest but his God's. His obedience to what he believed to be the will of God brought freedom to millions. . . . Wilberforce, by his persistence, but above all by the spiritual element at the root of everything he did, again and again made possible in the future what had seemed impossible when he first tackled it. Such is the statesmanship needed in his and every age" (*God's Politician*, p.183).

I pray to God that someone of this character will rise up and speak out soon.

Making a Necessary Statement

Never before in the modern Western world has the value of human life been so depreciated. Annually a million unborn but living children are slain through abortions. The ruthless slaughter of people portrayed in many current movies is cheered by their audiences. Proposals advocating different forms of euthanasia are given increasing support. In his book, *Against the Night*, Charles Colson speaks of "processes initiated . . . in government and the medical profession, abetted by unthinking citizens, [that] have already allowed inhumanities on a scale unimaginable only thirty years ago" (p. 52).

The teaching of atheistic evolution in public schools undoubtedly has contributed to the loss of a sense of the sanctity of human life. The "meism" so prevalent today contributes to our lack of concern about whether other people live or die. But whatever the cause, this diminishing regard for human life is destroying a major foundation stone of Western civilization.

Ultimately, all human rights issues are based upon the sanctity of life. Virtually every law that undergirds what we call civilized behavior derives from a belief in the sacredness of individual human existence. The Constitution of the United States is based upon a belief in man's inalienable right to live. We undermine social order and destroy the foundation of civility when we allow any erosion in our commitment to the inviolate nature of human life.

If there was ever a day and an issue concerning which Christians must "salt" the society in which we exist, it is this one. Our schools are not teaching this. The arts, which, generally speaking, no longer have a moral purpose, do not communicate the message. The media, with its constant search for the sensational, glorifies rather than disparages violence to persons. Government is seldom characterized by statesmanship that leads people out of error. The Church and religious institutions must deliver

117

the message that life is sacred. If it is not heard from that source it will be heard hardly at all.

One of the ways we can proclaim that message is by an obvious concern for the disabled and an aggressive program to affirm the value of such individuals.

A letter to the editor of the local paper of the city in which I live criticized money being spent for special education for persons with disabilities. Such persons, the writer argued, are unlikely to become productive members of society. Better, he said, to spend the money to accelerate the education of the brightest, most physically able students whose future leadership would give society its best return on its dollars.

One needs little imagination to see how such thinking could easily be extended to suggest that disabled people be done away with completely. Then money required for even their maintenance could be expended on the more promising specimens among us.

In the face of such Hitlerish ideas, Christians must protest that the worth of an individual is not calculated as a person measures the value of a used car. Civilized people who have a sense of responsibility to a God who made man in His own image do not treat the physically disadvantaged and the mentally retarded among us as animal shelters treat strays that no one will adopt. People who know that man is more than a physical being see beyond physical limitations to the precious human spirit.

And we can show that by welcoming people with handicapping conditions into our homes and into our churches. We proclaim that all life is precious by making whatever accommodations are necessary to admit such individuals into full participation in all our activities. We shout this to the world by helping the disadvantaged reach higher heights of achievement. We affirm the sacredness of life by showing love to those whose physical deficiencies may make them less attractive than the models who appear in fashion magazines.

There are other reasons why Christians should welcome in and minister to the disabled. But one good reason is the terribly needed statement this makes concerning the value of every human being.

Responding to the AIDS Epidemic

Recently, while I was watching a program on television about AIDS, some entirely improper thoughts passed through my mind. The program advocated a massive effort costing billions of dollars to find a cure for this disease. I confess to thinking, for a moment: *Why bother? Most of the people who are dying of AIDS are homosexuals or drug addicts. Ultimately society will be better off without homosexuality and drug abuse. Let them die.*

Apparently I am not the only person who has ever had such thoughts. Robert Twigg, writing in the *Mennonite Brethren Herald* magazine, made this assertion concerning individuals whom the general public sees as spokespersons for the Christian community:

> *I found in their statements . . . a moralistic, self-righteous superiority, based on the assumption that the true Christian would not waste his or her time with these lowlifes who had contracted this disease and had only themselves to blame for their suffering.*

But such ideas are unchristian. If anyone reading this has been tempted to think about AIDS victims in this way, let me urge you to reconsider. We must support efforts to find a cure for AIDS and do all we can for its victims.

Self-interest dictates that we care about a cure for AIDS. As increasing numbers of people become infected, the cost of their care is mounting. Most of those costs must be borne by the public. We should fight AIDS, if for no other reason, because of what it will increasingly cost us if it continues.

But there are far more Christian reasons for us to be concerned. Everyone who has AIDS is not homosexual. Not every victim is a drug user. Innocent people have contracted the disease through means other than sexual acts. Children are being born with the AIDS virus in their bodies. These people deserve whatever can be done to save them.

Even homosexuals or drug addicts must be cured if at all possible. The sanctity of human life is a fundamental teaching of Scripture and a basic tenet of Christianity. Any compromise concerning this principle undermines a foundational aspect of our faith. We, therefore, must do all we can to keep all human beings alive as long as we can. We must oppose any force or disease or practice that would take people prematurely to their graves.

When sin was introduced into the human race, God might have reacted as I did for that brief moment. The Lord might have said, "My creation will be better off without sinners in it. I will just let sin destroy mankind, and then this curse will be removed from the earth."

But the Lord did not respond this way. The Son of God came here to live among people infected with the deadly virus of sin. Moreover, He took that infection into Himself and died from it in order to provide a cure for sin that can be applied to our lives. To turn away, then, from AIDS victims and to say, "Let them die; they are only getting what they deserve," is to manifest an attitude totally different from that of Christ.

We must not only care about AIDS victims, we must reach out to them with help. Some congregations have ministries to alcoholics, to the homeless, to the hungry. Churches should establish ministries to victims of AIDS.

We should lend support to research and treatment programs. These cost a great deal of money. But money must never be more important to us than human life.

Obviously we cannot condone the lifestyles of homosexuals or drug addicts. Jesus did not condone the lifestyles of publicans and prostitutes. But this did not stop Him from reaching out in tender mercy to such individuals.

In A.D. 252 a plague broke out in Carthage. Many inhabitants of the area fled in fear, leaving the ill and the dying unattended. Cyprian, the Christian bishop, gathered his congregation, and these followers of Christ, at the risk of their lives, went throughout the city burying the dead and nursing the afflicted. This is Christianity in action, and our response to the AIDS plague should be no less Christlike.

The Curse
of War

Recently, I visited the Vietnam War Memorial in Washington, D.C. My wife and I joined the slowly moving line that filed past the thousands of names engraved in black marble. We passed people standing, staring at a particular section of the wall. We passed weeping relatives and some persons making tracings of certain names.

Not one of the dead memorialized there was special to me. I lost no close friends or relatives in Vietnam. But I could not keep tears from clouding my eyes and a large lump from rising in my throat.

I wept for every one of those precious lives cut down in their prime. I wept for the mothers and fathers who would never see their sons again, for children robbed of fathers, for homes with an emptiness that nothing can ever fill.

I wept for the casualties of the Vietnam War . . . and the Korean War and World War II and World War I and the Civil War and all the other senseless conflicts that darken the pages of human history. And feelings of frustration and anger rose up within me. With Tamburlaine, I cried, "Accursed be he who first invented war." War is the most insane of all human activities.

I am not debating the right or wrong of any particular country's involvement in any particular conflict. I know that sometimes wars are thrust upon us by others. I mean no disrespect to those who have been called upon by their governments to fight and have done so.

But the persons who start these conflicts and whose interests are served by them are not the ones who die. Choice young men (and sometimes women) are sent out like lambs to be slaughtered in sacrifice to the gods of greed and vengeance and ambition. Innocent civilians who ask only to be left alone are crushed and burned and torn apart by falling bombs and exploding shells.

This is the ultimate indication of the utter folly of mankind, that after centuries of life on this planet we still engage in the infantile exercise of killing each other in wars. Today, while I am writing this, people are being killed in battles. How utterly stupid we show ourselves to be. How completely ridiculous that we still think war accomplishes anything or that armed conflicts are in any way glorious.

I almost choked with emotion as I sat down on a park bench not far from the Vietnam War Memorial. I thought of the unspeakable brutalities people inflict upon one another in wartimes. I saw in my mind heaps upon heaps of dead bodies and red blood seeping into the soils of battlefields. I saw wrecked cities with smashed homes and piles of rubble.

I thought, too, of all the unfulfilled promises of peace offered by politicians, the innumerable conferences and treaties that have come to naught. Nations today are armed to the teeth. Tons of weapons continue to roll off factory assembly lines. And a sense of anguish lay heavy upon my spirit.

There will be more Vietnams. There will be more world wars. Men are as full of folly as ever. We still do not know how to live on this globe in peace. So senseless slaughters will continue. John Milton said, "For what can war but endless war still breed?" More, millions more precious lives will be lost. Grave will be piled on top of grave—unless and until . . .

God has promised us a Prince of Peace through whose government righteousness will cover the earth as waters cover the sea. Swords will be beaten into plowshares and spears into pruning hooks. "Nation will not take up sword against nation, nor will they train for war anymore" (Isaiah 2:4).

As I got up from that bench and walked away from the Vietnam War Memorial in Washington, a silent cry rose up within my soul:

Even so come, Lord Jesus. Come quickly. Please come soon.

The Inner-City
Poor

I have been haunted by something I saw a couple of years ago at Christmas in New York City.

My daughter, her husband and I attended a midnight Christmas Eve service at one of New York's large and beautiful churches. We celebrated there the coming of the Savior from heaven's riches and glory to identify with and to take upon Himself responsibility for our poverty and shame.

As we walked from the church building to our car, we saw about a half-dozen people lying in doorways of buildings and on sidewalks. Some were inside large cardboard boxes. Others lay under piled-up pieces of blankets and assorted rags, trying to protect themselves from the winter cold.

They were some of the hundreds of homeless that regularly sleep on the streets of New York City. Their number is increasing—and not only in New York. Growing numbers of homeless families are being forced to live on the streets of almost every city.

Homelessness is just one of the problems facing people in our inner cities. Malnutrition is common in some areas. Certain people do not have access to adequate medical care. Child neglect is too common in families. Poverty is contributing to the increasing incidence of drug use.

Today many evangelical churches are located in suburban areas, and people who attend these churches may never see the homeless and the disadvantaged. We are quite well provided for. It is therefore easy for us to ignore the problems.

But in doing this are we not rather like the priest and the Levite in Jesus' story of the Good Samaritan? Are we not guilty of "passing by on the other side" and neglecting people who are our "neighbors"?

Someone reading this may protest, "Those people are poor because they refuse to work. If they would get a job they would not have to live on the streets and go hungry." In a few cases that may be true. But the exceptions do not make the rule. In most instances people are disadvantaged because of circumstances, physical handicaps or mental deficiency over which they have no control.

Many of us feel that, in the past, government programs that have attempted to address such social problems generally have failed. Most of us would not endorse the idea that the answer to poverty and homelessness in America should be solved by new government programs underwritten by a large increase in our taxes. But if we are not willing to give government the funds to deal with these issues, does that not throw the problem back upon us?

I confess that I do not know what the church can do. I have hesitated to address this issue because I have no solution to propose. We can increase our support for inner-city missions and for organizations like the Salvation Army. But I doubt existing organizations have the facilities to cope with the mounting number who need help.

I do not know what the church can do. But it seems to me that we must do something.

At that Christmas Eve service in New York City we sang praise to God that His Son came down to the level of the humble and needy and poor. During His life among us the Savior turned aside to minister to a blind beggar. He fed the hungry. He went to the outcast. He mingled with lepers.

I am supposed to be a follower of that Christ. I am supposed to be like Him. Yet as I left a service in which I celebrated His coming, I walked past people sleeping under rags and plastic garbage bags on a cold sidewalk, and I did nothing for them.

I went back to the suburb in which I live, slept in a soft bed in a warm house, got up the next day to share an abundance of gifts and eat a sumptuous meal. And ever since I have wondered if I have any right to call myself a Christian.

The Tragedy
of Profanity

"O God! O, my God! My God!" Across North America these words are uttered millions of times a day—and not in prayer, not in preaching, not in praise. The blessed name of the sovereign Lord is used impulsively and frivolously to express surprise, concern, fear, delight or other such emotions.

Recently some children, boys 10 to 12 years old, were playing within earshot of my home where I was doing some yard work. Apparently these boys had discovered a large, ugly beetle and were tormenting it. In minutes the holy name of their exalted Creator rolled off their lips a dozen times, and it was used as casually as if they were invoking the name of a comic-strip character.

Radio airwaves and television soundtracks are becoming filled with this profanity. Many vulgar, four-letter words are still censored. But the sacred name of the Almighty is employed over and over in utterly irreligious ways.

To those who love the Lord, this trivializing and desecration of God's name is heartbreaking. Because I am seldom around smokers I am not accustomed to the stench of burning tobacco. Consequently, cigarette smoke assaults my nostrils violently. Perhaps it is because I do not hear God's name abused in my home or at the place I work that I am unusually sensitive to profanity. But I wince and feel inward pain every time I hear the hallowed name of Deity trashed by careless people.

There is no question about the sinfulness of profanity. The third commandment forbids the use of the names and titles of God in vain ways. Thus, if, as Jesus said in Matthew 12:36, men will have to give account on the day of judgment for every careless word they have spoken (and they will), millions, through careless use of God's name, are storing up for themselves much guilt for which they will have to answer.

However, there is another reason why the widespread vain

125

use of the Lord's name is so serious. The profane manner in which people treat God's name reflects a lack of respect for God Himself. One of my elementary school classes included a red-headed boy who despised the nickname "Red." And no one in the class ever called him that name, at least not to his face, because he was about a head taller than anyone else and the toughest guy in the group. Our fear made us careful.

A lack of awe toward God allows people to abuse His name. But how tragic, how serious! The fear of the Lord is the beginning of wisdom (Psalm 111:10). To the degree that we become increasingly irreverent toward God we become increasingly foolish. And that folly is undermining morality, destroying respect for life, fracturing the social order and leading society into ruin. The awful disregard for the sanctity of God's name by people around us is not some minor bad habit of an increasingly secular culture. It is a symptom of a tragic lack of reverence for the Creator that forebodes nothing less than our destruction.

Followers of Islam were enraged, and they protested and threatened violence against the author of *Satanic Verses* when it was published because they considered this book defaming to their religion. I hope I do so with less vehemence, but I am frequently forced to register my offense when I hear people profane the name of my God. And I think Christians have every right to be angry and to protest media standards that permit such abuse.

Beyond that, we ought to be driven to our knees in prayer for our land by the profanity that is all around us. Our society has not only turned its back on God, it now tramples His holy name beneath its feet as if it were no more significant than the words "fiddlesticks" or "humbug."

And one more comment: Christians should be exceedingly careful how we use God's name. I hear people who ought to know better using God's name in jokes, in flippant comments and passing remarks. We ought, by personal example, to rebuke profanity, not contribute to its proliferation.